Holy Writ

A Writer Reflects on Creation and Inspiration

Holy Writ

A WRITER REFLECTS ON CREATION AND INSPIRATION

K.D. Miller

The Porcupine's Quill

CANADIAN CATALOGUING IN PUBLICATION DATA

Miller, K.D. (Kathleen Daisy), 1951–
Holy writ

On cover: A writer reflects on creation and inspiration.
ISBN 0-88984-222-1

I. Title.

PS8576.I5392H64 2001   C814'.54   C00-933264-2
PR9199.3.M472H64 2001

Published by The Porcupine's Quill,
68 Main Street, Erin, Ontario NOB 1TO.
Readied for the press by John Metcalf; copy edited by Doris Cowan.
Typeset in Minion, printed on Zephyr Antique laid,
and bound at The Porcupine's Quill Inc.

Represented in Canada by the Literary Press Group.
Trade orders are available from General Distribution Services.

We acknowledge the support of the Ontario Arts Council,
and the Canada Council for the Arts for our publishing program.
The financial support of the Government of Canada
through the Book Publishing Industry Development Program
is also gratefully acknowledged.

1   2   3   4   ·   03   02   01

Canadä

Table of Contents

Introduction

According to my diary, I began work on *Holy Writ* in July of 1998. Since I finished the last essay in July of 2000, it might be fair to say the book was my millennium project. Except I didn't think of it that way. In fact, aside from collecting a few token canned goods and bottles of water, I didn't think much about the millennium at all. On December 31, 1999, I went to bed at my usual (early) time, then woke up at 12:01 to a racket that was nothing compared to what went on in this same Toronto neighbourhood the first year the Blue Jays won the World Series. I noticed my digital clock was still running, turned on a couple of lights to make sure life as I knew it would continue, then went back to sleep.

But I don't want to suggest that the dawning of the two-thousandth year since the alleged birth of Jesus had no effect on me whatsoever. The whole millennial decade, in fact, was marked with significant developments for me on both the spiritual and creative fronts.

In 1990, I joined a church. In 1994, then again in 1999, I contracted with a publisher to produce a book. However amused (or perhaps alarmed) each of those establishments might be by the suggestion that they have anything in common, in fact they have much. Each has a mission to the world. Each has a carefully refined idea of what constitutes 'good'. Each formalizes and brings out into the open what is initially impulsive and private. And each introduces the individual to a community of like-minded souls.

I've made good friends through both my church and my publisher. Over the years, my calendar has been dotted more or less equally with parish and PQL events. I have an ongoing relationship with both, and am grateful to both for their care and support.

But just as I did not begin to write when the senior editor of the Porcupine's Quill phoned me in 1993, neither did I suddenly acquire a religious faith in 1990 when an Anglican bishop put his hand on my head. In fact, I remember having brunch with a fellow writer in Guelph in the early eighties and confessing to him that I had just realized I was a default Christian. What I meant was, as a child of the fifties, I had been taken to church and subjected to daily Bible readings and the Lord's Prayer at school. As a result, whether I liked it or not, my worldview, my sociological makeup, a lot of my psychological baggage, were essentially Judaeo-Christian. Though it wasn't as fixed a factor as my race or sexual orientation, it was *there*, and it was bound to affect my writing. I was still an atheist, I hastened to reassure my friend, who had started to recoil. But a *Christian* atheist. Sort of. Did that make any sense?

It didn't, and I'm no longer any kind of atheist. I never really was, truth to tell, though at one time I did take non-belief in God to be a prerequisite for intellectual maturity. As for the Christian part, well, at some point things get *particular*. I speak a particular language and live in a particular place. By the same token, whenever I've felt the need to give shape and voice to my spiritual leanings, I've fallen back on my own Judaeo-Christian particulars.

This is not to say that I regard my religion as better, truer, wiser or inherently more valid than any other. As for those of my baptized brethren who do take the exclusionary view, all I can say is I'd rather be marooned on a desert island with a broad-minded atheist than a Christian fundamentalist any day.

So yes, I have been baptized and confirmed and I do have the certificates to prove it. But what I remember about both events is how utterly *human* they were. After my United Church baptism at age fifteen (which had more to do with a crush on a young minister and an urge to embarrass my Presbyterian parents than anything else) I floated around the house moony-faced for a couple of weeks before having to admit that life, and I, were essentially unchanged. My faith faded like a cut flower after that, and I began the long slouch toward atheism. I was almost there when I had that revelatory brunch in Guelph – about as close to an epiphany as I ever come. Shortly thereafter I began slouching the other way until, at thirty-nine, I ended up being confirmed on Easter Eve, 1990, in the Anglican Church of Canada.

There were about a dozen or so of us spiritual late bloomers that night. We were each given a white placard with our name printed on it, and told to walk, two by two, toward the sanctuary steps where the bishop sat enthroned. Each pair in turn was to kneel on the step right in front of him, holding our placards so he could say our names while placing his hands on our heads and reciting the rite of confirmation from the *Book of Common Prayer*.

It was every bit as simple as it sounds, and that was what worried me. I'm one of those people who can carry out complicated, even terrifying tasks with some degree of success; but give me one numbingly easy thing to do and I'll screw it up every time.

It didn't help that I was wearing a longish dress with an overlay of chiffon. I was convinced that when I tried to rise from the required kneeling position, my high heels would hook into the chiffon and I would roll backwards down the steps. I shared my fears with my partner, a woman named Valerie. She confessed to me that sometimes, when she knelt, her knees locked and she couldn't get back up.

Our turn came. Clutching our placards, we rose from our pew and approached the bishop's throne. Whether we would glide gracefully back from our episcopal blessing, or creep, scrunched and crab-like, was in the hands of God.

We knelt. And immediately heard a Voice. *Up one step,* it said in an urgent whisper. Was it the Voice of God, exhorting us to greater spiritual heights? No. It was the voice of the bishop. We had landed too low down for him to reach our heads. Unless we came up a little higher, he was going to have to tilt so far forward that he would likely fall out of his throne. And so, bunching up our dresses and juggling our placards, we clumped up one step on our knees.

'Defend, O Lord, this thy Servant (Valerie, Kathleen) with thy heavenly grace, that she may continue thine forever; and daily increase in thy Holy Spirit, more and more, until she come unto thy everlasting kingdom. Amen.'

My heels did not snag my dress. Valerie's knees did not lock. We made it back to our pew without incident, perhaps a little different than before, more likely much the same, but, as we agreed over sherry and goodies in the church hall afterwards, glad we did it.

Ten years later, I'm still glad I did it. I'm glad I was baptized at fifteen, too, whatever my immediate motive may have been. I don't for a minute think there was anything magical or permanently transforming about either experience. I don't assume they give me a special 'in' with God, and I know for a fact that they don't make me any nicer, kinder, gentler or more charitable than anybody else.

But both my baptism and my confirmation were a way of saying to the world, *This is who and what I am.* Or perhaps more accurately, *This is who and what I think I should be.* And I must confess that I feel an affinity for other people who have made a similar kind of statement. I sit up and take notice if someone is wearing a Star of David or turban or hijab. I'm intrigued by crucifixes hanging from rear-view mirrors, and was once delighted to look down out of a bus window into a convertible whose dashboard had a sticker on it proclaiming, 'I ♥ Allah.'

I may be wrong, but I believe we are by nature worshipful creatures. We sense in our bones that there is something bigger and better than our immediate circumstances, and we want to know and be known by it. I believe the creative impulse, the desire to make beautiful things, is a desire to be at one with our own Creator.

I remember the first time it occurred to me that writing fiction might be the way I pray. I don't remember the circumstances – where I was, whether I was alone or talking to somebody – but the sensation of several pennies dropping at once is one I'll never forget: So *that's* what compels me to write. So *that's* why traditional forms of prayer never work for me. I had suspected for a long time that the creative and spiritual sides of my nature were at least related to each other. But with that realization, I began to wonder seriously if one in fact *was* the other. Typically, I put the wondering in writing.

Holy Writ is neither a theological treatise nor an ad for Jesus. I lack the mental muscle for the former, and as for the latter, haven't an evangelical bone in my body. It was never my intention to act as an apologist for my particular religion. If anything, I think I set out to discover just how I manage to live with that religion, and whether I can continue to do so. At times it felt like marriage counselling, which does on occasion end in divorce.

Holy Writ is a neither a self-help book nor a writer's manual. It doesn't tell a prospective writer how to do it or where to sell it. I'm still working those things out for myself. Just as baptism didn't automatically render me Christ-like, publication has done nothing to solve the eternal problem of the blank page.

Holy Writ is one writer's exploration of how, in her own experience, creativity and spirituality relate to each other. Its approach is entirely intuitive, and I do not presume to speak for anyone besides myself. It is my hope, however, that the book will appeal not just to writers but to anyone who has an interest in the writing life. By the same token, while its reader does not have to be at all 'religious', I hope that what I have written here might resonate with any faith to which they do subscribe.

I am grateful to sixteen Porcupine's Quill authors who took the time to complete a questionnaire about their spiritual beliefs and writing rituals. Given that religion has become the ticklish topic that sex used to be, I had no idea what kind of response, if any, I would get. Well, I was overwhelmed. I heard from lapsed and practising Catholics, observant and non-observant Jews, three atheists, two Buddhists, one Quaker, a Native spiritualist and every sort of agnostic in between. My heartfelt thanks to Gil Adamson, Mike Barnes, Mary Borsky, Marianne Brandis, Melinda Burns, Elizabeth Hay, Steven Heighton, Cynthia Holz, Carol Malyon, Philip Marchand, John Metcalf, Peter Miller, Robyn Sarah, Antanas Sileika, Ray Smith and Russell Smith. Their voices greatly enrich this book.

For their interest and support, as well as a fascinating ongoing dialogue about art and the sacred, I wish to thank Leah D. Wallace and V. Jane Gordon. I am grateful to Chris Ambidge, editor of *Integrator*, for permission to quote from articles published therein; and to Sr. Thelma Anne, SSJD, whose essays about prayer, one of which I cite, have been a steady source of inspiration.

My thanks to the Porcupine's Quill for recommending *Holy Writ* for two Ontario Arts Council grants, and, on a more personal note, to Tim and Elke for always being there in so many ways.

Finally, I am grateful to John Metcalf, minister's-son-cum-reluctant-atheist, not only for doing double duty as editor and contributor, but also for convincing me that, yes, people just *might* want to read a book like *Holy Writ*. Thank you, my friend.

K.D. Miller, August 2000.

Morning Prayer

I write in the early morning. My alarm goes off at five, and I'm at my desk twenty minutes or so later, showered, dressed, coffee in hand. (I thought I'd dispense with that bit of news right away. People tend to react to it with anything from incredulity to rage.)

I discovered the early morning years ago. I say 'discovered' because it feels as much like a place as a time. My desk is lit by a single lamp, making me the sole inhabitant of an island of light. An island of silence, too, save for my barely whispered sounding-out of each word I write, like that of a child learning to read.

The need for silence was one thing that started me getting up at five in the morning. I was married years ago to a man who filled any and all silence with music – radio or records indoors, and out on the street, his own humming, whistling and singing. Fortunately, he liked to stay up late and sleep in, so I trained myself to do the opposite. I forget how long it took me to get into the early-to-bed, early-to-rise habit, but it's still ingrained, more than a decade after the divorce.

The other thing that led to my discovery was a short story written by Mavis Gallant – 'The Ice Wagon Going Down the Street'. In that story, a young woman confides to a man she hardly knows, 'When I was a kid I would get up in the summer before the others, and I'd see the ice wagon going down the street. ... That was the best. It's the best you can hope to have. In a big family, if you want to be alone, you have to get up before the rest of them. You get up early in the morning in the summer and it's you, you, once in your life alone in the universe. You think you know everything that can happen. ... Nothing is ever like that again.'[1]

Alone in the universe. ... Well, not quite. Just as the ice wagon goes down the street of that young woman's solitude, so does traffic noise come through the window of mine. From the hall, I can hear the elevator rising, then the *whump* of my newspaper landing just outside my door. And soon, in apartments above and below mine, clock radios will start to murmur, and showers to run. So I'm not so much alone as

13

undiscovered. Unsuspected. It's a bit exhilarating, almost like getting away with something.

You think you know everything that can happen. ... Sometimes. That is, if I'm ever going to gain some new perspective, see things with fresh eyes, it will be in these early hours, when my world is this small island of light.

Nothing is ever like that again. ... True. My handwriting never flows as evenly as it does first thing in the morning, when I'm still relaxed from sleep. My clean clothes are never as delicious against my clean skin. And although I'm single and childless and have one of the last jobs that actually fit between the hours of nine and five, as a writer I couldn't exist without this time set aside each day for silence and solitude.

The mornings give me something else, too, which is harder to name. I've looked for other words, better words, nicer words, but can't find them. So here goes. I need time, each and every day, to be selfish and lazy.

It may seem strange to attribute a regular discipline of rising at five and writing for two hours before leaving for work to selfishness and laziness. But let's do 'selfish' first. Those two hours are *mine*. I don't share them with or borrow them from or owe them to any other human being. Nobody pays me to set them aside, so I don't have to report to anybody what I accomplish in the course of them.

And that's where 'lazy' comes in. I don't even have to accomplish anything. Not in the normal sense of being able to point afterwards to something that wasn't there before – a page, a paragraph, a sentence, a single word. In fact, at the end of my morning time, what's there is frequently shorter than what was there the previous day. Or it might be all messed up with crossouts, arrows, asterisks and marginalia like *expand* or *contract* or *omit*. Sometimes it's completely unchanged, because all I've done is sit and read it over and over.

There are no rules for what I do in the early morning, aside from getting up and getting to my desk. And once there, there's nothing to keep me from day-dreaming about something completely unrelated to whatever I'm trying to write. Or staring at the wall. Or swivelling my chair and staring out the window, with a kind of despair, at the growing light.

I say 'despair' because pure selfish laziness is a very difficult state to maintain. I live in the world, after all, and it's a world that measures.

Counts. Sizes up. Prompts questions that I'll go on hearing as long as I go on writing. *How many short stories a year do you produce? What is your page-per-day quota? How long is a short story?*

How high is up, in other words. But when I look in despair at the growing light, when I think, *My time is almost over and I haven't done anything*, I am in effect asking those questions myself. And it's not as if I sit doing nothing, morning after morning. Writing is writing, after all, and the stories I've published did not write themselves.

Except they did, in a way. Any story must, to some degree, be allowed to write itself. It's a question of the writer knowing when to *do* and when to *be*. Or maybe when to let be.

Like the time I saw the angel on the balcony.

It was one of those mornings when I had achieved a state of almost perfect selfish laziness. I had given up all pretence of writing, wasn't even facing my desk, but had swivelled my chair and was looking out my study window.

Through that window, I have a view of my neighbour's balcony. My neighbour owns a huge grey Persian cat that she lugs outside in her arms sometimes to let him glare at me through my window. 'He'd love to know what goes on in that little room of yours!' she called to me once when I waved.

So would I.

Anyway, this particular morning, when I was gazing out the window, the balcony door opened and out stepped neither my neighbour nor her cat but a very beautiful, very naked young man. He stood with his back to me, the dawn light turning him pink. He had a gorgeous back, tapering down to a bum worthy of Michelangelo. I couldn't decide what I wanted more – for him to turn and see me, get the smile and friendly wave I was going to throw him, or for him just to stay the way he was.

Eventually, without turning, he stepped back inside, and I never saw him again. Not in the flesh. But I can never look out the study window without remembering him. And now, when I picture him in my mind, he has wings. Full, white, feathery angel wings. I know he didn't have them when I actually saw him. But he does now, and even if I wanted to I couldn't wish them away. They, and the beautiful back they're attached to, have become one of those hard little details that will rattle around in my imagination forever, like pebbles in a sieve.

The naked young man has already shown up in print, not just in this essay but in a brief article I published in *The Lazy Writer*.[2] And some day, in a story I have yet to write, a character will see an angel on a balcony. Or maybe he will actually *be* an angel on a balcony. I won't know until the time comes, and the time might not come for years. Decades. Not before tomorrow morning,

So the next time someone asks me if I start with a story outline, then work up a plot synopsis and character sketches, maybe I'll just tell them that what I in fact do is sit and stare out the window until a naked man shows up and grows wings. It will be my definitive answer to that eternal (and eternally tiresome) question, *Where do you get your ideas?*

Actually, I wouldn't mind being asked that question if the emphasis could more often be on the words *you* and *your*. Most of the time, though, it's on the word *ideas*, as if the questioner believes there is a great mother lode of fresh material out there, just waiting for anybody with the right map, the right method, the right substance, the right teacher.

Well, I have some good news for them, and I have some bad news.

The good news is that, yes, this El Dorado of ideas does exist. And yes, there is a map showing me how to get to it. And yes, there is a substance that will heighten my perception of what I'll find once I've followed the map. And best of all, yes, there is a teacher who will tell me exactly how to extract and refine all the glittering ore that will be mine for the taking.

Now for the bad news.

The map traces the route between the coffee maker in my kitchen and the desk chair in my study. The method consists of sitting on that chair. The substance is coffee with milk, no sugar.

And here comes the worst news of all.

The teacher is me.

Not that there aren't excellent professional teachers of creative writing out there, and useful workshops to attend, and retreats to come back from feeling rejuvenated and refreshed. Also, I greatly value the friendships I've formed over the years with other writers. God knows, you need something to balance the essential solitude of the writing life.

But that's just it. *Essential solitude.* There's no getting away from it, save by giving up writing. And for me, that isn't an option. Those early hours are sacred time. That island of light is holy ground. Writing stories is the way I pray.

I haven't always seen things that way. I haven't always wanted to. For years, I attempted atheism, largely because I craved its intellectual cachet. I sometimes still do, when it comes out in conversation that I go to church, and the person I'm talking to gives me that sugary, seraphic smile that means they've pegged me as one of the not terribly bright.

It's unfortunate that the imagination and the intellect are so often assumed to be at odds with religious faith. I assumed as much myself, even after being 'outed' as a Christian by a friend and fellow writer. We were part of the same writing group that met once a month. The group had just set the date for the next meeting, a Friday in April. My friend turned to me and, with the air of broaching something terribly delicate, asked, 'Will that be all right for *you?*'

The date in April was Good Friday. He had noticed a certain consistency of imagery in my writing, and had drawn a conclusion that was more accurate than I was prepared, at the time, to acknowledge.

I now suspect that my own awareness of what my friend could see so clearly started to dawn well before that incident. And I think my habit of getting up at five in the morning was more than a reaction to my husband's noisiness, or to that story by Mavis Gallant.

Like most boomers, I was taken to church each Sunday throughout my childhood and adolescence. Then, once in university, I quickly learned to curl my lip at anything that smacked of organized religion. I'm still not sure why, at the age of thirty-nine, I started sneaking into an Anglican mass on Sunday mornings. I was so terrified of being seen doing this supremely uncool thing by anyone I knew that I travelled blocks out of my way to get there, walking briskly, head down, just stopping short of ducking behind trees.

I could only remain incognito for so long. One by one, the faces in the pews lost their uniform strangeness. A nod became a 'Good morning,' then an exchange of pleasantries, which grew into an actual chat during Coffee Hour. My cover was finally blown on Name-Tag Sunday, when, teeth gritted (because I hate name tags), I obediently printed K.D. MILLER on a sticker that announced cheerily to the world, HELLO MY NAME IS.

Over the years, I've managed to unclench my teeth long enough to become a somewhat black-sheepish member of my church family. (It's a flaw in my character that if I could figure out a way of having communion without community, I'd do it.) But I've served on a few committees. Sometimes do the reading during a service. Donate clothes to the Christmas bazaar. And yes, I'm glad to be part of a congregation. I like the way the Sunday service punctuates my week.

And yet. And yet.

When somebody from the church phones me to ask if I'll do some job that needs to be done, I'm equal parts flattered and dismayed. Flattered, because there's a side of me that bustles, that organizes, that sees to and makes happen. Dismayed, because there is another side that wants to be anonymous again, to sit silently through the service, alone and unknown. Whatever it was that dragged me back to an exercise of regular worship at the age of thirty-nine, it was not Coffee Hour. I don't go to church to be on committees, either. Or to read the lesson aloud. Or to help with the Christmas bazaar.

I go to be selfish and lazy.

I go to see the angel on the balcony.

I'm starting to discern a pattern here.

Writing stories is the way I pray. I've been telling myself that for years now. But what exactly am I talking about?

At various times in my life, I've tried out more traditional forms of prayer. I've meditated on lit candles, run mantras through my head, even toyed with the idea of setting up some kind of prie-dieu apparatus to kneel at. Overall, I've found the whole business to be frustrating and embarrassing. And it's always been with a mixture of guilt and relief that I've given up and gone back to what I *can* do, namely write stories.

But how can the two activities be compared? Isn't there something fundamental about prayer that shows up the, well, the *phoniness* of fiction? I thought so for years. Then it occurred to me that to search for the right word is to search for the word that tells the truth. And the struggle to portray a character honestly, that is, free of cliché or stereotype, is a struggle to love that character.

I may be wrong, but I am very skeptical of some authors' claim that they write 'pure' fiction – that is, made up out of whole cloth and containing none of the stuff of their own lives. Perhaps I'm imaginatively stunted, but I can't conceive of doing such a thing, or of wanting to. When I'm working on a story, I am, however obliquely, examining my own fears and failings and joys and hopes. If that isn't praying, I don't know what is. And surely the attitude of writing, with its surrender of conscious control and its willingness to wait in silence, is identical to the attitude of prayer.

Be still and know that I am God.[3]

That has to be one of the tallest orders ever given. And one of the most terrifying. Which may account for the contrast between the jam-packed schedule of activities pursued by many churches throughout the week, and the one wee hour accorded to worship on Sunday. It may also explain why some writers enrol in one course or workshop after another, attend every book launch, reading and literary event in town all year long, yet do very little actual writing.

It's an easy trap to fall into, this state of perpetual distraction. I've fallen into it myself, in the last couple of sentences. Because what I *want* to say, what I am trying to say is so damned difficult. Dangerous, even.

There. Dangerous. That's it. Prayer, whatever form it takes, is not Prozac. And I know I'm doing my best work when what appears on the page scares the hell out of me. When what I've just put in writing for all the world to see is the very secret I've been keeping from the world. And from myself.

It doesn't have to be earth-shattering, or horrifying. It can be very small and simple, even, to other eyes, inconsequential. But it is *true*. Its truth can throw me for a loop, can shift my perspective by the single degree that will change everything. Whatever it is, whether tiny or huge, it's paydirt. Its danger lies in its capacity to turn pages and pages of overworked prose, perhaps even the work of a lifetime, into so much fool's gold.

No wonder Saint Paul wrote that we must each work out our own salvation 'in fear and trembling.'[4]

But enough of the soapbox, or pulpit, or whatever it is I've perched myself on. Actually, it's my desk chair. The coffee's all gone, and the light coming in the window is bright enough that I don't need my lamp any more. Time to go get the newspaper. Glance at the headlines and the weather. Read an article or two while I have my toast. Then look at my watch, say, 'Oh my God,' and start rounding up what I need for the day – purse, lunch, keys, shoes.

Morning prayer is over. But as I rush out the door, the angel on the balcony folds his wings and waits.

---

1. Mavis Gallant, 'The Ice Wagon Going Down the Street', in *The Oxford Book of Canadian Short Stories in English,* selected by Margaret Atwood and Robert Weaver (Oxford University Press, 1986), 130, 133.

2. K.D. Miller, 'The Best Place to Write', *The Lazy Writer,* 1, no. 4 (Winter 1998).

3. Psalm 46:10.

4. Philippians 2:12.

Travels with Harold[1]

'We stole away because we wanted for the love of God to be on pilgrimage, we cared not whither.'

In this way, according to the Anglo-Saxon Chronicle of 891, some Irish monks spoke to King Alfred after they had landed in Cornwall in a boat without a rudder.[2]

This anecdote cracks me up. I think it's the phrase 'without a rudder' that does it. I picture the scene of the monks landing on a Cornwall beach as a cartoonist – perhaps George Booth – would draw it. There is King Alfred, arrayed for the Royal Dip in boxer trunks, flippers, polka-dot inflatable rubber horsey-thing, and crown. He regards the monks with that look of indignation kings always give anything that perplexes them. For King Alfred, as much as any king, does not like to be perplexed. He likes to know what's going on. And he likes to be in charge of it.

In this, he is in greatest contrast to the monks, half a dozen or so of them, sweetly alike in their robes and tonsure, crammed into the rudderless dinghy that has brought them to the sovereign's flippered feet. The monks regard Brother King much as they would Brother Beggar or Brother Tree or Brother Jackass. They too are perplexed by what has happened. But unlike the King, they don't *mind* being perplexed. They're used to perplexity. Feel quite at home with it. It is akin to wonder and to humility, states of being which comprise their stock-in-trade. In fact, by setting out in a craft they could not control, choosing as their destination 'we cared not whither' and giving as their reason 'the love of God', they can be said to have been *courting* perplexity.

Not to mention oblivion, as I'm sure the King wastes no time pointing out to them. Disaster. Dampness, at the very least. And all the while, the monks smile up at him and happily agree.

* * *

Whenever I write a story, there is part of me that is the King and another part that is that cluster of questing monks. And as long as I go on writing, the two factions will disagree as to the right way to be on a pilgrimage.

'Pilgrimage' is defined in part as 'a journey, especially a long one, made to some sacred place as an act of devotion'.[3] That may not sound as if it has much to do with the writing of fiction, but I think it does. I believe writing is, among other things, a spiritual exercise. Not that it has to involve belief in the supernatural or the formal practice of some religion. On the other hand, when I try to articulate what it *does* involve that might be considered spiritual in nature, I have a problem.

'Spiritual' has become a buzzword. Politicians and advertising executives have jumped onto the 'spiritual values' bandwagon. Social commentators speak of a generalized 'spiritual hunger' arising from the decline of organized religion and the growing dissatisfaction with consumerism. In order to discern what *I* mean by spiritual, I have to rid my mind of all that and just try to concentrate on the word itself. But when I do, I feel as if my head is filling up with dandelion fluff and a space is appearing between my feet and the floor.

One thing that could anchor me if I let it is my own religion. I do have one. I attend a weekly worship service where I hear the word Spirit used in the context of the Trinity: Father, Son and Holy Spirit. In recent years, in some churches, the Trinity has tried to become a little less paternalistic by renaming itself Creator, Redeemer and Sustainer. But the effect, of a curiously categorized deity, is the same.

It doesn't help, either, that when I was a child the Holy Spirit was called the Holy Ghost. Whenever I heard that phrase, I used to picture an anaemic-looking wraith named, for some reason, Harold. Harold the Holy Ghost was one of those folks who mean well and try hard but lack anything resembling talent. He trailed after God and Jesus in my imagination, desperately trying to look like part of the team, but never actually being given anything to do.

I owe a debt of gratitude to mystery writer Dorothy L. Sayers, for rescuing the Trinity for me from utter absurdity. In her book of essays, *The Whimsical Christian*, she relates the whole thing to a work of art.[4] First, she says, there is the artist, the creator of the work. Then there is the work itself, whether a painting or a piece of music or a poem. This work of art, given life by its creator, has a life of its own, too. A presence. A spiritual dimension with which we can enter into a kind of communion.

I enter into just such a communion whenever I'm reading a story or novel which suddenly, uncannily, is all about me. In a way that has nothing to do with the particulars of character or setting or plot, it becomes *my* story. It seems actually to *know* me, as well or even better than I know myself. And by the same token, though we have never met, though one of us may indeed be long dead, the author and I *know* each other.

This jolt of recognition is one I have heard described in many different ways. I would best describe it in terms of its effect on me, which is pure wonder.

Is that what I mean by 'spirit' and 'spiritual', then? A sense of wonder? A true sixth sense that gives meaning to what the other five perceive? That discerns in all created things, including myself, the essence of the Creator?

If so, it would certainly give Harold the Holy Ghost something to do all day. And I can imagine the monks in their dinghy being buoyed by just such a sense of wonder. At least, I can't imagine them embarking without it.

I don't think their pilgrimage is over, either, or that Cornwall is their sacred place. In fact, if I'm going to relate this anecdote to the writing process, I would have to say that Cornwall is no more than the first leg of the journey, one the monks will look back on rather wistfully. For it is at Cornwall that the King insists on coming along. And bringing his map. First ordering the Royal Boat-Builder to affix a rudder to the stern of the dinghy. A rudder whose tiller the King, needless to say, will control.

So the little craft once more puts out to sea. As land drops from sight, the monks send up prayers that with (or perhaps in spite of) the King's help, they will reach their God-chosen sacred place.

* * *

But I'm getting ahead of myself.

'We stole away ...' That's the first thing the monks confess when they land in Cornwall. *We stole away* ... I love that phrase. It captures the furtiveness of writing, which for me is one of its main attractions.

To begin with, writing is perhaps the most solitary of the arts. It is a silent activity that can be hidden from curious eyes by an arm crooked round a page, and whose tangible results can very often be folded and tucked into a pocket. Try *that* with a tuba, a corporate-art sculpture, or a full-cast production of *King Lear*.

But what's so attractive about all that solitude and secrecy? *We stole away* ... There's something illicit in that phrase. After all, you only steal away *from* something that, if it knows you're leaving, will try its damnedest to make you stay put. The monks stole away from their monastery. Their order. Their abbot. The rules and routines that governed their intensely communal lives. They did physically what I do psychologically when I write – steal away to a place where I can follow my own rules and live up to my own expectations.

If this is sounding selfish, it is. And I happen to think the word 'selfish' has received some undeservedly bad press. For as the monks say, 'We stole away *because we wanted for the love of God* to be on pilgrimage.' In other words, they abandoned their religious duties and their religious community for profoundly religious reasons.

I abandon my entire life for an hour and a half every morning when I go to my desk to write. During that time, I'm not allowed to pay bills, check my e-mail, brood about family and friends or think about the looming work day. I say 'not allowed' because I have had to make strict rules for myself about all these activities. As innocent or even commendable as they may be, they are insidious. They will invade my solitude if I give them an inch, move right in with all their clutter and crises, discover my plans for a pilgrimage and chorus together, 'But you can't *possibly* be thinking of leaving *now!*'

And so, like the monks, I must steal away. For the love of God. Whatever that is. Again, I should know, because I hear it talked about every Sunday. But what I hear every Sunday is that God's love is unconditional and everlasting. Well, I'm afraid I can't quite take that in. Not that I've never loved or been loved. But I am a finite and fallible creature, and my love experiences have involved other finite and fallible creatures. And even the best among us falls far short of loving everlastingly or unconditionally.

So what good thing *is* there in my life that I could describe in those terms? I would have to say, the creative impulse. It has always been there for me, one way or another. As a child, I lived to draw pictures. In my teens and twenties, I dreamed of being an actor. It was only in my thirties, when I started publishing stories, that I realized I had always written, if only as a substitute for drawing or acting when those other activities were letting me down.

Whatever form it takes, the creative impulse itself never lets me down. It gets me out of bed every morning and pulls me to my desk. If the time comes when I can no longer get to a desk or hold a pen, I know I will still feel and respond to that impulse, if only by spinning stories in my head.

* * *

'... we cared not whither.' It's one thing not to know where you're going. It's quite another thing not to care. And with regard to the writing process, I have come to think of not caring as an achievement. In fact, the less I care where I'm going with a story, the more likely I am to get there.

This is not to say that I am totally indifferent to the final shape of a work. Nor do I mean to deny the King his due. For there is a point in the process when in effect somebody has to say, 'All right, just what's going *on* here? What's the *plan?* What exactly are we trying to *do?*' But it is very important not to start out that way, and not to want to get to that point too soon.

How does a story start? Every writer would answer that question differently. I'm going to begin by describing how, for me at least, a story does *not* start.

It does not start with me saying to myself, 'I'm going to write a story about a man whose ex-lover is dying of AIDS.' Nor does it start with me saying to myself, 'I'm going to write a story about a man whose ex-lover is dying.' It doesn't start with: 'I'm going to write a story about a man with an ex-lover,' either. Or: 'I'm going to write a story about a man.' Or even: 'I'm going to write a story.'

Which is why I can be struck dumb by that perfectly reasonable question writers get asked: 'What are your stories *about?*' Someday I'm going to learn to intone some hifalutin nonsense like, 'The ineffability of human experience,' and hope that it strikes the questioner dumb. But until then, I'm going to twitch and grope for words, probably giving the impression my books were ghost-written.

The problem is, I don't write *about* anything. *About* just doesn't come into fiction writing, as far as I'm concerned. I remember once being asked by a radiologist who had read my first book, 'Why did you decide to write about AIDS? Breast cancer kills just as many people in North America, and you *are* a woman.'

This challenge presupposed many things: that as a female author I have an obligation to address women's issues; that any story which I write must perform some kind of task, like informing the public about breast cancer; and again, that I consciously set out to write 'about' anything.

I don't remember what I said to the radiologist. But what I should have said is, 'You're referring to the title story of my first book, *A Litany in Time of Plague.* I didn't decide to write about AIDS, or any other disease, however topical. I never make such decisions, at least not consciously. Instead, a story in effect sneaks up behind me and taps me on the shoulder.'

Actually, it starts with something very like a vision. No, I don't go into a trance or hear voices or anything like that. It's more a case of not being able to get something out of my mind. A gesture. A snatch of dialogue. Whatever it is, it almost always involves some *body* as opposed to some *thing* or some *place.* I hardly ever adopt the omniscient point of view. I much prefer working behind the mask, through the gritty particularity of character, with all its abrasive limitations. The more unreliable a narrator promises to be, in fact, the more likely I am to let him tell his own story and bend it completely out of shape. Three of the stories in *Litany* are narrated by Raymond Mayhugh, a man so entirely self-absorbed that he has yet to make his own acquaintance.

In the case of the story that piqued the radiologist, it started when I kept imagining Raymond curled up in foetal position in his bedroom closet. This piqued *me,* because it was the last thing I could imagine the deeply shallow Raymond doing. So I waited, and in time, he began to tell me what was going on.

I realize this sounds a bit spooky – almost as if characters have lives of their own. All I can say is, they do. Though they are without doubt creatures of the imagination, characters are not puppets. They aren't mouthpieces for the author's political or philosophical views, either, or blunt instruments for bludgeoning her personal bogeymen. They command respect, and have something to teach their creators. I once heard Margaret Laurence tell an interviewer that Hagar Shipley, the old woman who narrates *The Stone Angel*, just walked into her head one day and wouldn't leave.

Something like that happened to me with Raymond Mayhugh. He showed up for the first time in the story 'Author Of' as a relatively minor character, then proceeded to make it his own. All I could do was follow him around and take notes. Which I'm very glad I did. If I had dug in my heels and kept him in his place, I would have ruined the story and undermined my own development. As it is, Raymond taught me a lot.

But enough of what the writer said to the radiologist. Or wishes she had. I have stolen away, because I want for the love of God to be on pilgrimage. Now what?

Good question.

* * *

One of my dirty little secrets is that although I have written short stories for years, I haven't a clue what a short story is. That is, I could not stand at the front of a classroom and chalk onto the blackboard three defining characteristics of same. Or two. Or even one. How short is short, anyway?

Now and then I get worried about my ignorance and thumb through a how-to-write book, where I usually find some kind of definition. I read it, marvel at its clarity and wisdom, then promptly forget it. And go back to writing short stories. Whatever they are.

I must confess to taking how-to-write books, and creative writing courses, with a grain of salt. There are some excellent ones out there. There are others that are pure snake oil. I tend to avoid any book or course that tries to sell me some 'system' for releasing my inner whatever. The kind that tells me to spring from my bed before dawn, go directly to my desk, write a single word in the middle of a piece of paper ('coffee' no doubt, or perhaps 'bathroom') then word-associate in a circle around it, counter-clockwise, in order to stimulate the right side of my brain. Or is it the left? Maybe the bit in the middle.

It isn't what I'm being told to do that makes me suspicious so much as the fact that I'm being told to do anything at all. I just don't think there can be a system for creating a work of art, any more than there can be a system for falling in love, or a system for being happy. It occurs to me that I'm equally suspicious of religious sects and religious leaders that offer quick fixes for life's problems, or pat solutions to life's mysteries.

A good piece of writing is a mystery. No matter how revised and edited and polished it may have been, it appears in its every detail to have been not so much contrived as *destined*. Fated. Meant to be. That is, the words on the page are the only words that could possibly be there.

But how do I find those words? How do I arrive at that sacred place?

First, by trying to keep the King out of the boat as long as possible. I know I'm going to wash up at his feet eventually. But the more rudderless drifting I can do, unencumbered by map or compass or timetable, the more likely I am to get some inkling of my final destination.

I do a lot of staring into space at this stage. Daydreaming. Pulling up old, familiar memories and trying to look at them with new eyes. Keeping my eyes open when I walk to work, and my ears open when I ride the subway.

I do some writing too, come to think of it. But it's an idle sort of writing. Just bits and scraps and fragments that may or may not have anything to do with each other. Sometimes a phrase or a sentence will catch me like a current and carry me along for a while. Right now, though I'm not actually writing any fiction, I'm very taken with two sentences: *How do you find somebody you can barely remember? Where do you start to look?* I haven't a clue what those sentences are about, or what, if anything, they might lead to. A family saga? A murder mystery? No idea. But I run them through my head now and then, and every time I do, I feel a thrill of possibility. I suspect I could have tremendous fun with them sometime soon.

And that's the most important thing of all. Writing, at this stage, must be fun. An adventure. It should have nothing of work or duty about it, and should be totally unencumbered by rules or expectations. Because all too soon, the happy, aimless journeying does have to end. The King, a.k.a. the conscious mind, a.k.a. the internal editor, must be allowed to impose some kind of game plan.

So begins the most difficult and dangerous part of the pilgrimage. Difficult, because it involves a dialogue (more like an argument) between the conscious and the subconscious. Dangerous, because it is so easy to lose sight of the original intention, which was, again, *for the love of God to be on pilgrimage, we cared not whither.*

It's a time of tiny heartbreaks. Of labouring for weeks on a paragraph, then looking at it one morning and realizing that it simply has to
go. Or of suddenly remembering a passage that I threw out weeks ago
because it was useless, irrelevant, going nowhere. But now it's become
vitally important, central, the very heartbeat of the piece. So where is it?
How did it go? What were those words again?

And then, in the middle of all the bickering and confusion,
somebody yells 'Land ho!'

* * *

The ending of one of my stories can be as much of a surprise to me as to
anybody else. It can suddenly just *be* there, when I could have sworn I
had pages and pages more to write. It can be utterly different from anything I had imagined. Which is why I can sometimes fail to recognize it.

I now realize, for example, that the story 'Egypt Land' which appears
in my second book *Give Me Your Answer*, should have ended with the
words, 'So preoccupied, he sat down.' In fact, I remember thinking so at
the time of writing. But I was too in love with some rather precious sentences that had been running through my head all the time I worked on
the story: 'He became Old Pharaoh, and the Sphinx and the pyramids.
He became the wind and the sand and the pipes and the drums and the
incense and the sweet oils. He became Egypt Land.' So that's how the
published story ends, all tied up with that pretty bow.

Oh well. We live. We learn.

In the case of 'Sparrow Colours,' I did get the ending right. In that
story, Daisy Chandler is living with a man whose child she has recently
aborted. The experience has made the man realize that he wants to settle
down, marry Daisy and have children with her. She, however, has come
to the opposite realization. At the end of the story, knowing that what
she is about to do will destroy their relationship, she blurts out, 'I killed
my child, and I'm glad I did it. I don't mourn it. I don't miss it. I don't
want it back. I don't want to replace it. And if I have to kill another one, I
will.'

Those words scared me. I couldn't accept them at first. I kept trying
to soften them, warm them up, sweeten them. Finally I realized what I
was doing. I was trying to make my heroine (and by extension myself)
nicer, kinder, less threatening, easier to like. I was trying to be popular.

And what does popularity have to do with the love of God?

Whether I liked them or not, Daisy's final words had the unmistakable weight of inevitability. They were the sacred place to which the story had journeyed. All I could do was lift my hand from the tiller and drift in to shore.

---

1. Brief sections of this essay originally appeared in my article 'Learning to Write Big', published in *The Capilano Review,* Series 2:16.

2. Philip Sheldrake, *Befriending Our Desires* (1994), 122.

3. *The Random House College Dictionary,* revised edition (Random House, 1984).

4. Dorothy L. Sayers, 'Toward a Christian Esthetic', in *The Whimsical Christian* (1969).

An Act of Will
and an Act of Faith

ROBYN SARAH

I feel my work as a writer to be, before it is anything else, a kind of spiritual office, a devotional act. I have known this about it for so long that I cannot remember when I first framed the thought; it is almost as though the knowledge was there from the beginning (which cannot be the case, because I began writing at the age of six. I was certain from that age that I would 'be a writer when I grew up' – a conviction from which I never swayed, though there were times when I thought I might be other things as well, and in fact I have been).

I do know that when in my early twenties I began reading the journals and letters of writers and artists whose work I loved – (Katherine Mansfield, James Agee come immediately to mind) – I felt a powerful sense of recognition (and amazement) when I came upon passages in which they spoke of their art in similar terms. (Agee in a letter to Father Flye, February 1936: 'I care mainly about just 2 things ... They would be (1) getting as near truth and whole truth as is humanly possible, which means several sorts of 'Truth' maybe, but on the whole means spiritual life, integrity and growth; and (2) setting this (near-) truth out in the clearest and cleanest possible terms ...' And Mansfield, December 15, 1919: 'At the end *truth* is the only thing *worth having*: it's more thrilling than love, more joyful and more passionate. It simply can*not* fail. All else fails. I, at any rate, give the remainder of my life to it and it alone.' And elsewhere, she prays in her journal to be made 'worthy' to write the story she wants to write: 'Lord, make me crystal clear for thy light to shine through.') I felt they *spoke my language,* and that there was a mysterious affinity, or communality of spirit, among artists in general – an affinity

---

Montreal poet and short story writer Robyn Sarah is one of sixteen authors who responded to my questionnaire concerning the spiritual aspects of the writing life. Hers was one of four responses I chose to reproduce in full.

that transcended generations, cultures, and languages – almost a 'religion' of art. It was such a relief to discover that there were others who had been where I found myself, that it was a real place in the world, that I was not the only one.

But I have not found it possible to make Art my *only* religion. I have a private, complicated, often ambivalent, but necessary and nourishing relationship with my religion of birth (in my case Judaism) – this though religion played almost no role in my childhood.

A conflict: it is my nature to value my anonymity, and to embrace solitude. I want to hold apart and be quiet. Christianity, I think, gives the reclusive impulse some room: at least it has a monastic tradition. Judaism has none. Judaism is a religion in which prayer is in the first person *plural,* and certain prayers, important in the liturgy, can only be recited in the presence of a *minyan* (quorum for prayer). As a faith and a culture, Judaism is relentlessly communal, claustrophobically so for someone like me. Also problematic is that aside from the artisanal, Judaism has no artistic tradition (probably stemming from the commandment regarding graven images). As a religious culture, it tends not to appreciate or understand art except as illustration: the concept of 'art for art's sake' is foreign to it.

So I'm a divided soul. I can't 'not write', but I could never renounce my Judaism. I need both, and they can't be reconciled. Both are essential to my being, but in my heart of hearts I know I can't be both at the same time. It's a somewhat schizophrenic existence. (Cynthia Ozick once said in an interview that at the moment she sat down at her desk to write, she ceased to be a Jew. I know exactly what she means.) It's not a situation I'll ever be happy with, but I've accepted it as my lot, as who I am, as how I was made – and the closest I can come to reconciliation is to tell myself that I have a spiritual obligation to be true to who I am, in the fullest sense, and therefore I must not deny the writer in me, but pursue the writing as purely as I can. (There's a story I love, about Rabbi Zusia: he said,' "At the end of my days in this world, if they will ask me, 'Why were you not Moses?' I will know what to answer. But if they will ask me, 'Why were you not Zusia?' – what excuse shall I make?'")

Have you at any time experienced a significant change in your

religious outlook, whether through conversion, loss of faith or some-
thing that might be called an epiphany?

Epiphanies, moments of grace – yes, they happen – little ones, almost
every day. When they don't I figure the fault is mine: it is because I am
not paying attention.

'Significant change in religious outlook.' At the age of twenty or
twenty-one I had a kind of revelation: that I should be able to *sweep the*
floor in the same spirit that I wrote a poem, and write a poem in the same
spirit that I swept the floor. To sweep the floor (a 'humble' task) with the
same devotion that I give to writing a poem; to write the poem (an
'exalted' task) with the same humility one feels when sweeping the floor.
I guess that is still as close to a personal spiritual credo as I can get. It
shows that by twenty, I already felt there was something 'religious' about
my writing. The revelation was twofold: that the exaltation of writing
needed to be tempered, or it risked becoming vanity; that the most
mundane task could be elevated to a devotional act if it was performed
in the right spirit.

Does ritual play a role in your writing life?

I don't have a conscious writing ritual, just habits. I do usually have
coffee at my elbow and I prefer to face a window. Looking out of the
window is important. I keep a journal, and often begin a writing session
with it, usually (but not invariably) starting with the view from the
window. (There's a lot of weather in my journal.) I make periodic
attempts to set myself a writing schedule (ideally, I like to be at my desk
before it gets light in the morning), but I've never been able to stick to
one. I write whenever I manage to get up the nerve to sit down to it – I
do find it takes nerve.

Would you apply the words 'holy' or 'sacred' to your writing time,
space or habits?

If I did, it could only be ironic (as in explaining why I should not be
interrupted). 'Holy' and 'sacred' aren't words I normally use at all.
Actually, I feel that if anything, I need to demystify the act of my own

writing, to keep it simple, not to make it into something bigger and more intimidating than I already feel it to be. It is an *act of will and an act of faith* for me to sit down to write (this applies to poetry and fiction, but not to journalism: journalism is just another task, more enjoyable than some, but basically a form of floor-sweeping). I say an act of faith because I never know whether anything is really going to happen, and so much seems to be staked on it, and so little seems to be in my conscious control, and that's so scary.

> *Is inspiration a necessary part of the creative process for you? How would you define inspiration? Where does it come from? Are you in control of it?*

Yes, inspiration is terribly necessary. I can't define it but I know when it's absent. I'm inclined to consider it a form of grace. No, I am not in control of it. (I wish I were.) All I seem to be able to do is to keep myself *open to it,* which seems to mean *paying attention* – a kind of listening, but not just with the ear : with the whole being. When my writing is going well, I feel as though the actual words come from a source outside of me. They are 'given' to me. I become a conduit. (This seems to be particularly true for beginnings and endings.)

> *Do you need, as well as want, to write?*

At one time, I thought that if somebody were able to tell me with a certainty that I would never write again, I would not want to live. I don't know if I would put it that way now, but I do find it hard to imagine why I would ever get up in the morning if I did not think it possible that I might write something today. I have always felt writing poems and stories to be my primary purpose in life, even when I have not been actively engaged in it (I have *long* 'dry spells' – more than a year at a time, if you don't count my journal and letter-writing and journalism as really writing: I don't).

> *Do you believe that our society needs for you to go on writing?*

Absolutely not. It is *I* who need for me to go on writing. And my poems

34

and stories seem to *need to be written* (but in their own sweet time). But given this compulsion to devote the best that is in me to this one thing, I feel an imperative, in order that the act not be completely selfish and hermetic, not to *hoard* the writing but to share it. Which means that little as I like the business of seeing that the work gets into print, I feel an obligation to see that it does. (To be worthy of sharing, the work had better be good. So I try to make it good. How good? Let's put it this way: If they will ask me, 'Why were you not Tolstoy?' I will know what to answer. But if they will ask me, 'Why were you not Robyn Sarah?' what excuse shall I make?)

Rendering unto Caesar

For most of my adult life, I've been an accidental employee. That is, the work I've done to earn my living has usually been the last thing on earth that under normal circumstances I would choose to do.

'Normal circumstances' refers, of course, to that perfectly reasonable fantasy we writers have of a little packet of money – not too much, just enough – appearing at regular intervals in our bank account, not in payment so much as in recognition of our having faithfully sat at a desk for at least a few minutes every day, pen in hand, staring at a wall. Life, however, does not always live up to even our most modest expectations. Society sometimes fails to see us as the National Treasures that, deep down, we know ourselves to be.

Hence, the day job.

'Day job' is a curious phrase. Is writing my 'night job'? Do I come into my own after the sun goes down, like a literary vampire? If so, that makes my day job the coffin to which I must return at sunrise in order to survive. Well, there are times when it feels that way. Even though I don't in fact write at night. I get up at five in the morning to give myself two hours at my desk before I have to start thinking about work.

Work. Now, there's a word that earns its keep. I was once married to an actor who did temp office jobs between shows. Whenever we ate out, he and our waiter would more often than not recognize each other from the audition circuit. My husband would be loosening the hated tie required by whatever office had hired him that week. Our waiter would be rushing around serving us and six other tables. And all the time they'd be moaning to each other about the fact that neither of them had any 'work'.

For some reason I've never adopted that euphemism. So I can be a bit slow on the uptake when a fellow writer asks me if I'm 'working'. *Well of course I am,* I almost say, referring to my day job. *I've been working for twenty years. Monday to Friday. Nine to five. With pension and benefits and some hope of parole in 2016.*

In all fairness, I guess writing does constitute the hardest work I do, in terms of concentration and commitment. It just doesn't feel that way to me. Once when I was showing a friend my apartment, I took him into the study and said, 'This is where I play.' Quite reprovingly, he came back with, 'No, this is where you *work.*'

But I wasn't trivializing what I do in that room. I get very irritated when child psychologists presume to justify play by calling it 'the work of childhood'. How dare they? Play is a lily of the field. It requires no more justification than a sunset or an orgasm. If anything, it's *work* that needs to be justified. Or at least, the punitive psychological baggage we've loaded it down with.

... only by the sweat of your brow will you earn your bread ...[1] So God says to Adam before kicking him out of Eden where he probably got into trouble in the first place because he didn't have enough to do. But if you take those words out of context, they can as easily be a blessing as a curse. Imagine a deity saying sternly to a writer, *Only by sitting in a chair, thinking very hard and writing down your thoughts will you publish!* Most of us would reply, 'Cool! Where's the chair?'

Work-as-punishment, or worse, work-as-ethic are two notions the world could have happily done without. Give a child a task and watch how quickly he turns it into a game. It's an instinctive alchemy that artists remember all their lives, but the rest of the world largely forgets.

Years ago, a neighbour of mine told me she felt sorry for me. When I asked her why, she said that sometimes on a Saturday morning she would pass by my apartment door and hear me typing. I had worked all week, she knew, and she didn't understand why I couldn't just relax and enjoy myself on the weekend.

I did try to explain that writing was the most relaxing and enjoyable thing I knew how to do. But I doubt I convinced her. And for my part, I am often puzzled or even repelled by what the rest of the world considers fun. White water rafting? Video games? Decorating patio table tops with smashed bits of crockery? Are we all mad? If I ran the penal system, inmates would be forced to choose between Scottish country dancing and macramé. The recidivism rate would drop like a stone.

* * *

I've *worked,* that is, I've been hired to do jobs and have had a social insurance number, from the age of sixteen. But again, I've almost never worked for the sake of the job, but to support some habit – school or acting or writing.

Which may be why, when I look in the mirror, I experience a split second of disbelief. I just don't *feel* like what I see. In reality, I'm less than half as big, and am clutching for dear life a blob of Plasticine or a crayon or a plastic cow – some indispensable part of the world that is my creation. It's up to me, each and every morning, to make the world all over again. I have to hurl myself at my play farm, my construction paper, my paint box, and try to finish before the grownups tell me it's time to eat or take a nap or take a bath or go to bed.

Or go to work. Disguised as one of them.

It's a good disguise, and a good act. I was a theatre student for hundreds of years, and in the summers would find myself cast as everything from a bank teller to a playground supervisor.

The costume for the latter job included a T-shirt with the word RECREATION marching across my breasts in bold red letters. I had props, too – a whistle that I blew sometimes through tears, a bunch of keys, none of which opened the one padlock on the playground, and a series of forms to fill out with headings like MEDICAL EMERGENCY and CRIMINAL ACTIVITY. The only thing I didn't have was a script. Every day was a nine-to-five improvisation, featuring all the children in the world, all screaming to be centre stage at once. It was my first job, and it forced me, at sixteen, to be more grown-up than I've ever had to be since. Most days, I was the only adult in sight, towering like Gulliver over my charges, who managed to be in charge of me.

One afternoon, when I couldn't stand it any more, I divided them into teams and sent them off on a scavenger hunt with a diabolical list that included six four-leaf clovers and seventeen red hairs. (I had checked first that none of them had red hair.) Well, they must have found a strawberry blond and plucked him bald, because they were all back within ten minutes with everything on the list, demanding to know what the prize was.

But during those blessed ten minutes of peace, I entertained a fantasy I'd been having since the summer began. It involved a room containing nothing but a desk, a chair and me. It was absolutely quiet in that room save for the sound of my breathing, and absolutely still save for the movement of my hand across a piece of paper. The fantasy puzzled me, because what I wanted to be at the time was an actor, and the last thing I associated with the theatre was peace and quiet. But years later, after some doors had shut and others had opened, I read *A Room of One's Own* and the penny dropped. Ever since, any job I've had, any money I've earned, has gone to pay the rent on that room.

It's a playroom. Its literal counterpart is my study, which contains not just a desk and a chair, but all the toys I managed to salvage from my childhood. They're crowded together in an antique cradle where they watch me, button-eyed, while I play.

* * *

I hope I'm not getting precious here. I really don't think the world owes me a living. However I might feel about the work ethic, I took it in with my ABC's and it's part of my blood and bones. I'll probably never entirely shake the notion that toiling away at something I'd rather not do is somehow better for me than work I enjoy. That it puts starch in my spine. Stiffens my resolve. Thickens my skin. I can't quite put my finger on what's so good about all this stiffening and thickening, but I believe in it anyway.

Still, the fantasy I described at the top of this essay, of a kind of writer's stipend or pension, is one that I do, on a certain level, take seriously. I haven't a clue how such a thing could be administered. But deep down, I feel it to be justified.

It's the child in me, of course. The necessary child who must be nourished and encouraged to play. And just as it never occurs to a child to question his right to his morning bowl of Cap'n Crunch, or wonder if he shouldn't perhaps get a part-time job to help pay for it, my inner child can't understand why, every day, she must pretend to be an adult and go to work.

As a result, part of me has never really settled in to the job I've had for twenty years. I do it. Sometimes I even do it well. I count my co-workers among my friends. But every morning, there's an inner tantrum I have to allow to play itself out before I can push away from my writing desk and get ready for work.

Does everybody feel this way? Sometimes in the morning on the bus I look at the faces and wonder if every one of them is masking some tiny grief for a garden, a child, a book or a musical instrument they've had to abandon till the end of the day.

There's nothing for it, of course. The world is what it is. All I can do is try to follow a remarkably practical bit of advice to *render unto Caesar the things that are Caesar's and unto God the things that are God's.*[2] And hope and pray that I always know which is which.

* * *

Years ago, I spent one summer as the world's worst bank teller. It was in the days before computers, when we actually had to tot figures up, Bob Cratchit-style, on a huge balance sheet. Well, I never balanced. Not once. Every single day, the accountant and I would toil overtime, trying to figure out what I had done wrong. I have a painful memory of no less than the manager on his knees, pawing through my waste-paper basket, trying to find a cheque for five hundred dollars I vaguely remembered getting from somebody that day. Or maybe it was the day before.

Toward the end of my brief financial career, I wrote to my acting teacher to bemoan the fact that *moi,* a budding *actrice,* should be so *malheureuse* as to be stuck *dans un banque.* Or words to that effect. He wrote back to point out that plays, generally speaking, are not written about acting students. They tend more often to be written about people who work in banks. People who lead lives of quiet desperation the like of which I was being given a chance to experience, if only for a short time. The summer would soon be over, and I would be back at university again. In the meantime, I had the opportunity to render a service.

The opportunity to render a service ... Very true. And very wise. And probably the most sensible and mature way to handle the necessity of the day job.

There's just one problem. I don't *want* to render a service. I want to *play.*

Hence my compartmentalized existence. Again, I get up early, write, then go and do the job that pays for the writing. At times, it feels like a supportive but passionless arranged marriage. I'm not ungrateful for the situation. I know it could be a lot worse. My 'husband' is even a little more interesting than most.

I work for a major charity where, as part of a small staff, I train and interact with a large number of volunteers. Recently when my editor

41

phoned me at work, he signed off with, 'I'll let you get back to doing good.' Yes, there is a whiff of altruism in the air of the place. We are non-profit, after all, and though the volunteers don't wear haloes (one of them admits she comes to us to get away from her rotten kids once a week) the bottom line is that I am surrounded every day by people who work for something other than money. Which rings a bell for me, as a writer of short fiction.

But *twenty years...!* When I filled out all the personnel forms in 1979, I believed I was going to work there for a maximum of six months. Just long enough to be noticed by the right director at the right audition. Or at least get my foot in the publishing door. Two decades later, I've left the stage (actually, it left me) and my foot is still just inside that door.

Maybe I'm kidding myself, presuming to keep the day job at arm's length. How can you do anything for twenty years and be unaffected by it? The furtive bits of writing a mother might manage during the twenty years it takes to raise a child does not keep her from being a mother. Composing haiku while serving a twenty-year jail sentence does not make a convict any less a convict. But neither does parenthood or prison necessarily make a writer any less a writer.

So why do I work so hard at keeping my writing and my working selves separate? Maybe because they're showing signs of wanting to get together. Maybe because I'm starting, almost against my will, to get fond of the 'husband' I did not choose. Maybe because there were days when even T.S. Eliot banked for the sake of banking.

As I've been writing this, the word *community* has been nudging the back of my mind. *Community.* Such a tired, worn-out, overused and misused word. I am increasingly seen as a member of the *literary community* – a contradiction in terms if ever there was one. Not that writers are necessarily unfriendly. It's just that we tend to peer at each other from around corners, over barriers and between slats. We're not, generally speaking, joiners.

A few years ago I found myself in a room full of writers I had gotten to know through The Porcupine's Quill. Our mission that day was to be cute and charming for the benefit of a group of sales reps our publisher was pep-talking in an adjoining room. While we waited, we began to tell each other about our childhoods. Without exception, we had been misfits and maladroits. Bullies' delights who had stood on the edge of the crowd, or tagged along behind it. We all admitted to being heartily relieved that this part of our lives was over, and that we had learned, more or less, to fit in. To lead what might be called normal lives as employees, spouses, parents. But we also, without exception, expressed gratitude for the experience of being marginalized. It had turned us into watchers. Listeners. And that distance, that separation from the community, however once so painfully imposed upon us, was something we now respected and maintained, for the sake of our writing.

So yes, there is a part of me that is pure lone wolf, a solitude junkie who agrees with Sartre that hell is other people. But there is another part that, willy-nilly, rubs shoulders with people – nice people – every day. And it would be dishonest of me to say that the only benefit I derive from my day job is money.

When you've worked anywhere for twenty years, you pick up a certain amount of authoritative lint. I'm the one who remembers where we put whatever we're looking for back in '87. Who knows that we already tried that procedure back in '92 (or was it '93) and it didn't work then and here's why. At staff meetings eyes turn to me – I like to think for affirmation or confirmation – but more likely just to see if the Ancient One is shaking her feathered rattles at some newfangled notion.

Tomorrow is Monday. It's also my birthday. Curiously enough, though I usually don't go in on Mondays till one, I've been asked to show up an hour early for a 'special staff meeting'. At that 'meeting', there will be a pizza and a cake and a present and a card. The card will be signed by people I've worked with for two or five or ten or fifteen or, in one case, twenty years. Crammed onto that bit of folded cardboard will be references to my writing. Cracks about my new haircut. Reprises of office in-jokes that I couldn't possibly explain here or anywhere else.

These people *know* me. They've known me married and divorced. They've seen me slim down and fatten up. They've helped me decide to curl it, spike it, grow it out then cut it all off again. They were there when I published my first short story. My first book. My second book. I've modelled outfits for them, then taken their advice on what to wear to book launches, readings and literary awards dinners. They've seen me laugh, cry and lose it. I spend more time with them than I do with my family or my best friend. I spend more time with them than I do writing.

So what is that? A community? I suppose. A family? Of sorts. A kind of love, I guess. I didn't seek it out, but it's there anyway.

And let's not forget the opportunity to render a service. For which I am grateful.

I think.

––––––––

1. Genesis 3:19.
2. Matthew 22:21.

Looking for Yahbba

I am a WASP. I am also heterosexual, middle-class and middle-aged. A few decades ago, all that would have constituted having the keys to the kingdom. (Though as a woman I would have still been missing the most important key.) Today, quite rightly, those attributes have been stripped of much of their social status and put back in their place as, well, attributes. Accidents of biology and geography and time, with a little luck stirred in.

That said, I think there's an important difference between, for example, acknowledging that the balance of power between men and women is still far from even, and condemning all men for being men. So I do not subscribe to the school of thought that dismisses William Shakespeare as a Dead White European Male, or refuses to listen to Puccini because the plot of *Madame Butterfly* is racist or sexist or whatever it's held to be this week. It's a matter of distinguishing the baby from the bathwater. And I worry that a lot of perfectly good babies have been going down the drain in recent years.

One of them is my religion. Attending a Christian church, I know, constitutes supporting an institution whose history is marred by the suppression of women and the abuse of minorities. The same thing is true, however, of engaging a lawyer, using a bank, attending a school, calling the police or paying one's taxes. Nobody's hands are clean. But for some reason, though the crimes of other institutions are conveniently forgotten, the villainy of churches lives on. The hour-long Sunday service I attend is enough, in the eyes of some people, to put me slightly to the right of Genghis Kahn and make me accountable for the Crusades, the Inquisition and every religious atrocity since.

In addition to shouldering global guilt, I am expected, by virtue of being a believer, to unlock the secrets of the universe. I'm routinely asked why, if God exists, he doesn't get up off his ass and *do* something about the mess the world is in. I've learned there's no point in suggesting that, since human beings are largely responsible for that mess, perhaps they should get up off their own asses. All I get is another

45

rhetorical question: *Well, why didn't God stop us from making the mess in the first place?* What I should say at these times, but never remember to, is: *Go ask the mother of any two-year-old.*

Then there are the folks whom my churchgoing causes the same embarrassment that used to greet the most oblique reference to one's sex life. I have some inkling of what homosexuals go through with friends and associates who *just don't want to know.* Or with voyeurs who *do* want to know, but are curious (yellow). I have one of those, who occasionally asks me if I'm *still* going to church, as furtively as she might ask if I'm *still* wearing leather underpants.

Though I can see the funny side of all this, I resent the way it puts me on the defensive. Because quite frankly, my baptized brethren worldwide can embarrass the hell out of *me* at times. I roll my eyes as far back as anybody else's when some televangelist is caught with his pants down and his hand in the collection plate. A phrase I've come to dread in newspaper headlines is 'Christian family values', invoked as often to defend the beating of children as anything else. I'm as outraged as any humanist when some Bible-belt 'Christian coalition' lobbies against gay rights, reproductive choice or the teaching of Darwinian evolution in the classroom, all in the name of a Jesus who had not one word to say about any of the above.

I know it's all so much bathwater, but it's very hard sometimes to salvage the baby. Or even find the baby. Or just believe the baby is there.

After all, what do I have to go on? An army of Christian soldiers renowned for shooting themselves in the foot. A gut feeling that I call *belief* but that many a psychiatrist would dismiss as wish-fulfilment. And finally a book in whose pages I find accounts of murder, rape and ethnic cleansing comparable to anything I'll read in the newspaper, and carried out in the name of a God who most often resembles Hannibal Lecter in a Santa suit.

* * *

Which brings me to that most dysfunctional of families, the Father and the Son.

'Abba, Father,' he said, *'all things are possible to you; take this cup from me. Yet not my will but yours.'*[1]

46

These words are spoken by Jesus in the Garden of Gethsemane the night before the crucifixion. Boiled down, they amount to a man begging his father, who is in a position to do so, to save him from an agonizing death. Then adding, in effect, 'But if you really want it to happen, it's okay by me.' It doesn't help that *abba* is the informal form of *father* and would have the sentimental weight in Aramaic that *daddy* has in English. It doesn't help to know in advance how the story ends, either. Because the way that story is written, it doesn't so much end as evaporate.

No matter how it's related or depicted, the resurrection of Jesus from the dead is just too magical, too fantastic, to be convincing on a gut level. Throughout the gospels there's something basically disappointing about the risen Jesus' appearances to his followers. He's back again, but not to stay. He's with them, but not of them. Freshly bereaved, they must lose him again. Thomas is allowed to touch him only in order to realize that painful truth. [2] Mary Magdalene is forbidden to embrace her beloved. [3]

This simply does not add up to the 'happily ever after' the child within us craves. So no wonder we're still hung up, so to speak, on the nails. No wonder crucifixes most often depict Christ not leaping triumphantly up and away from the cross, but still pinioned horribly to it. Because that's where his daddy wanted him to be.

Why does Jesus give this 'daddy' the time of day? Why do I, for that matter? I don't have to, and for years I didn't. But my attempts at atheism have always been exercises in self-deception. If there is such a thing as a *theistic* personality, I seem to have one. I tend to look for connection, order and meaning. Even if I can't find them, I like to think they're there somewhere, hidden from my short-sighted view. I believe in God, in other words, because I *want* to.

All right then. But why struggle with the difficult, subdivided Judaeo-Christian God? Kinder, gentler religions are available. The New Age movement offers the ultimate in user-friendly spirituality. For that matter, I could just go through life as so many people do, claiming to believe in Something, but too busy and distracted to give much thought to What.

Well, for me that would be like being too busy and distracted to breathe. And again, though my own religion is awash with bathwater, I would at least *like* to believe there's still a baby in there somewhere. I am, historically, sociologically and psychologically, bent into the shape of a Christian. Even as a writer, I'm imaginatively hooked on the Jesus story. My adult choice to be confirmed was a spiritual 'coming out'. An acknowledgement of what I am.

But being and doing are two different things. How do I practise my faith, given the realities of Judaeo-Christian religious literature? How do I even read a book that is so curiously hinged in the middle? What has the New Testament to do with the Old? More specifically, what has Jesus' *Abba* to do with *Yahweh*?

I can't conveniently ignore the Father and adore the Son, though I have tried to do so. But it's so hard to see any family resemblance between the two, and so easy to suspect Jesus of making excuses for the Old Man out of admirable but misplaced loyalty. In order to accept unquestioningly Yahweh's every action and recommendation, I would have to be in turn a racist, imperialist, homophobe, male chauvinist and hypocrite. Though the last is certainly within my grasp, I flatter myself that the rest are a bit beyond me.

So what am I to believe? Was Jesus a remarkable, but remarkably deluded young man who projected his own magnificent personality onto an unworthy deity, then called it Daddy? Or was that very magnificence a window onto the true nature of God? If I choose to believe the latter, then what am I to do with the leftover bits of Yahweh I would rather not think about — the rigidity, the precise keeping of accounts, the bewildering savagery?

I need to reconcile what appear to be two utterly opposed gods. I need to find, in an awesome creator/destroyer whose back Moses was allowed to view but whose face, if glimpsed, would have turned his own to ash, [4] some vestige of the 'Daddy' recommended by Jesus. I suppose I am looking for Yahbba.

* * *

There was a time in my life when God was as plainly and simply real as my parents or my house. The stories I heard about this God in Sunday school were as firmly based on fact, I believed, as the ones I heard about Christopher Columbus, or about my grandparents.

When I started to read seriously, at the age of ten or so, I was fascinated by myths and legends, by tales of Odin and Manitou and Zeus.
Still, I understood (or thought I did) that these stories could not possibly pack the same theological punch as what was in the Bible. Other
races and societies might very well have their gods; but *my* god was *God.*

At some point, it must have dawned on me that there was something
wrong with that picture. I don't remember any great awakening, and
certainly no battle in my household. My parents took my brother and
me to church throughout our childhood, then, once we were in our
teens, decided to sleep in on Sundays and let us figure it out for ourselves. And it was the sixties, after all. The Beatles had already declared
themselves more popular than Christ. By the time I got to university and
met Nietzsche, I was thoroughly contemptuous of the faith of my
fathers, and quite prepared to agree that God was dead.

Well, for the last decade or so, I've been trying to reverse that process.
I want to gather up all the knowledge and experience and psychological
baggage I've accumulated and, in a spiritual sense, take it home. I want
to go back where I came from.

* * *

The Old Testament account of the journey from Eden to the Promised
Land of Canaan is the story of a whole nation trying to go back where
they came from. It starts with the harmony of Eden, then the discord of
the fall; the slow, difficult bonding as God and humankind try to
reconcile; the enslavement and liberation from Egypt; the refining of a
national character, changing the apathetic slaves of men into the united
people of God; finally, the. decisive crossing of the Jordan, and the
confrontation with destiny at Jericho.

Like all great myth, this story has the power to resonate with my own
spiritual journey. At the same time, it is a violent, often horrifying tale,
the kind that prompts rhetorical questions starting with, *What kind of
god...*

Well, that's exactly where I'm going to start. With that question.
What kind of god would in effect 'write' the Old Testament?

Let's first eliminate what kind of god Yahweh *isn't.* He is not a silent
partner. He is not an absentee landlord. He is not a deadbeat dad. What

49

he *is* is intensely, even excruciatingly, involved in his creation. He watches its every move. If it puts a toe out of line, he's right there, bellowing abuse in its face.

Drill sergeant is only one of many analogies I could draw. *Quarterback* and *Old woman who lived in a shoe* also come to mind. My personal favourite is *artist*. More specifically, *temperamental artist*.

* * *

If they could, the characters in my stories would probably describe me as a holy terror, an almighty *She* who gives them life one day, wipes them out of existence the next, and changes her mind six or seven times in between about how they look, what they do for a living, their gender and sexual orientation, etc. I doubt very much they would realize that *She* loves them. But I do. I want them to be as fully alive as they can be in the best story I can write. This makes every story I write, whatever its content, a love story. And it ensures that every story I write begins in 'Eden'.

My creative Eden is both like and unlike the one depicted in Genesis. It's not so much a place as a state of mind, from which my story and I inevitably 'fall'. It's not of my own making, this Eden, because I can't, as God does in the first creation account,[5] make something out of nothing. My creativity is more like the clay-modelling and garden-planting that goes on in the second account.[6] But even in this I'm severely limited. Just as I can't make the materials I use, neither can I inspire myself to use them. Unlike the divine creator, I have to sit around and wait for inspiration to come to me from somewhere else.

It can come at any time, in any form. An unremarkable bit of conversation overheard on a subway platform might haunt my imagination for a day or a year before I see it for what it is. A stale childhood memory might be suddenly freshened by something I glimpse out the window of the speeding train. One way or another, I come to know that a story is starting up. I have no idea what it's going to be about. I just know that I'm going to write it.

This is my Eden, this delicious combination of excitement, curiosity and uncertainty. The trouble is, I never stay there for long. As soon as my pen touches paper, the story and I 'fall' together, alternately cursing and blessing each other on the way down.

Our 'fall' does not come about because of anything we've done or neglected to do. It's just the nature of the creative beast. The second I start to act on an idea, something of that idea is lost or obscured in the necessary containment of energy by form. And from that moment, I have to struggle to hold on to the original inspiration. I have to 'remind' the story over and over of what gives it life.

Something about that rings a bell. One of Yahweh's Old Testament habits that has always irritated me is his breathing down the necks of the Israelites – his pouncing on every tiny deviation from his long list of rules. It's an oppressive, old-fashioned management style, guaranteed to bring out the worst in people.

But maybe that's the point. The Israelites are people. They're an obstinate, forgetful bunch in the painful process of becoming the people of God. They're as separate from their divine creator as a story struggling to be written is from the memory or insight that first animated it. So in both cases, the neck-breathing is necessary. It's a process of refinement by which the worst is indeed brought out, in order to be done away with.

Which gives the fall from grace a creative dimension. In the writing of fiction, without the 'fall' from conceptual to concrete, there is no story. Similarly, in the Old Testament, without the expulsion from Eden, there would be no Genesis, no Exodus – again, no story. No 'memory' of Eden, hence no striving toward Canaan. No struggle to reach out to God across a divide. None of the heartbreak and joy that mark such a struggle.

This is serving to answer a question that has nagged me for years, namely, why doesn't God just let Adam and Eve stay in the Garden? What is the point of putting the serpent there? In other words, why not create automatons incapable of independent thought? Why imbue human beings with free will, if exercising it makes all hell break loose?

Well, maybe original sin is something other than just a practical joke played by Yahweh on the hapless tenants of Eden. Maybe it's the essence of our human nature, the thing without which we would not be human, and the human story could not be told. (Or at least, wouldn't be very interesting. Anybody who's suffered through English 100 knows there's exactly one entertaining moment in *Paradise Lost*, namely when Satan touches down.)

But where was I? Oh yes, my wonderful idea and I were taking that slow, bruising tumble into prose.

Unlike God, I haven't the slightest idea what I'm doing in terms of plot. If I happen to start a story at the beginning, I haven't a clue how the thing will end. If I start at the end, I'm at a loss as to how I got there. And if I start somewhere in the middle, I can't imagine where I came from or where I'm headed. All I can do is try to remember Eden and hope and pray to end up eventually in Canaan.

This is a far cry from divine omniscience. And unlike the unchanging God, I learn and grow as my creation takes form. It's debatable sometimes whether I'm writing the story or the story is writing me. It's a power struggle. For all my good intentions, I weigh my story down with irrelevancy and mediocrity. I despair of what it (what I) might have been, and hate what it (what I) have become. I want to rip it up. I want to stop writing altogether.

I almost do. But then I don't. I save one page. One paragraph on that page. One sentence of that paragraph. One phrase. All right, let's try for one word, shall we? A name, in fact. *Noah.*

Managing to find 'Noah' in all that I've scribbled and crossed out is a very humbling experience. Whatever form he takes, Noah is the stuff of Eden. He breathes the original inspiration. He reminds me of what the story is about, what any story is about. More, he reminds me of why I write.

I write in order to pray. Writing is how I talk to God, and how I listen to God. That's why the whole business is so difficult. And so precious.

So I resolve to be very careful with Noah. I won't risk losing my temper with him again. I'll just let him float away in his ark for a while, becoming a dot on the horizon. He'll let me know when to seek him out.

If it is presumptuous, this seeming empathy with God, it comes of my having finally caught a glimpse of the face of Yahbba. As an artist, I can understand both the love and the rage; the impulse and the regret. I can understand the need for time out, too, when God procrastinates a little before 'remembering' Noah in his ark.[7] As a dear friend once said to me, 'A lot of writing gets done while you're busy making banana bread.'

Whether or not the deity is in fact creating banana bread while Noah floats away is not recorded in scripture. But the time comes at last to put an olive leaf into the beak of the frantic, searching dove, to let the waters inch down, and to make a rainbow in the sky.

Sometimes, when I write, I go through a period of what I can only call grace. The story writes itself at these times. My pen or keypad can hardly keep up with the words I seem to be 'hearing' in my imagination. The original inspiration breathes every phrase into life, and it is all very good. At these times, the story and I are in Canaan, as close as we can come, after the fall, to being back in Eden.

As I reread the Eden-to-Canaan story in the Old Testament, it seems to me that the character Abraham ushers in such a period of grace. The relationship between God and creation is intense but loving. This close, parental involvement on God's part continues throughout the lives of Isaac, Jacob and Joseph. The story is immensely readable now, and the characters marvellously realized. They are fully human – complicated, fallible, always ready to exercise the gift of free will by wrestling with their creator. In time, they manage to wrestle their way out of Canaan and into Egypt.

In the Old Testament story, the route to Canaan is in fact marked by one Egyptian detour after another. It's possible that, in the collective imagination of the people of God, Egypt might constitute an alternative destiny. After all, Egypt offers a steady job and abundant food, right here and now. Canaan, on the other hand, is a long-term goal, attainable only through struggle and sacrifice. The Promised Land is just that – a promise.

And at first, Egypt is very good to God's people, keeping the budding nation from starving, nurturing and protecting it for generations. But in time, the host becomes the captor. The employer becomes the enslaver. If Israel is to survive, it must get out of Egypt and find its way back to Canaan.

The same thing happens with every story I write. It starts during that period of grace, when the work is virtually singing itself to me. I have a feeling of déjà vu that convinces me I'm tapping my subconscious, hearing an old, old song that has so far come to my conscious mind only in single notes and phrases.

Well, I'm wrong. What I am in fact hearing is the safe, lulling music of mediocrity. That feeling of déjà vu has nothing to do with my subconscious, and everything to do with the best-sellers I'm imitating. I've drifted out of Canaan into Egypt, and now I'm stuck there.

Writers speak of finding their voice – a process that takes years, and is marked by false starts. *Canaan* is the story written in my own hard-won voice. *Egypt* is the story spoken, in effect, by a ventriloquist's dummy. It is derivative and dishonest. *Canaan* is fresh. It has a disturbing edge. It risks alienating its reader. *Egypt* is reader-friendly to a fault. It is to *Canaan* what Muzak is to Mozart. *Canaan* is the story as it is meant to be written. It is a promise I have made to myself. *Egypt* is that promise broken.

So far, I've never once managed to get straight to Canaan without at least one detour into Egypt. This makes me appreciate suddenly the degree to which hindsight informs the writing of the Old Testament. The psalmists grew up knowing that their people had escaped slow death in slavery. The words *In the beginning...* were inscribed by someone who had at least glimpsed the Promised Land, and knew the cost of that promise's fulfilment. To put it simply, the writers of the Old Testament wrote from journey's end.

My own writing, in contrast, is more like a travel diary kept by somebody who hasn't a clue where she's going. I stumble along, as blinkered as the Israelites of old. Like them, I put down roots trustingly in Egypt. Like them, I take my sweet time realizing that something has gone terribly wrong. Once I do though, there's only one person I can blame, and one person I can turn to. First I have to admit to being my own Pharaoh. Then I have to find some way to be my own Moses.

In this necessary creative struggle, I begin to see the rationale for God's first letting the Israelites settle in Egypt, then extricating them with such pain and difficulty. The pain and difficulty of the exodus are all part of the refining process. The enslavement and liberation constitute a deliberately planned crisis, intended to awaken, unite and strengthen the people of God.

I wish I could claim that much strategic intelligence as a writer, but I can't. I end up in Egypt by accident, by losing sight of what I'm supposed to be doing. But when I do manage to extricate the story and get us both back on the road to Canaan, the feeling is indeed one of personal liberation. Salvation might not be too strong a word. I am forced to examine why I write, what I write for, and, in that light, to decide what I will and will not allow the story to do.

This is my Mosaic law. Keeping it means crossing out, crumpling up and throwing away any vestige of Egypt, including the diverting subplot or charismatic character that got us there. It is a heartbreaking process. I dream up one golden calf after another, then have to trash it. The story and I do battle with each other for what feels like much longer than forty years.

But we have no alternative. We remember Eden. We have seen the Promised Land. There is nothing for it but to make every detail reflect both visions. It is a terrible time, and an exhilarating one. Characters die. Others walk in out of nowhere and take over, because they are right for the story. A Moses gets left behind while a Joshua is hastily groomed to lead the story across the Jordan. Unjust? Maybe. But creation is a mystery. It will not be reduced to a set of platitudes or a schoolyard-level concept of fair play.

So if the bloody conquest of Canaan as recorded in the Book of Joshua appals me, if I turn momentarily cynical over Israel's flouting of God's commandments not to kill and not to steal, I can only remind myself that I too wreak violence on the page for the sake of bringing the story to its necessary conclusion. Its holy end.

* * *

Meanwhile, back in the garden ... Gethsemane, that is. Not Eden. Though I'm starting to see that the two have a lot in common.

... all things are possible to you; take this cup from me. Yet not my will but yours.

Does every story I write in effect say that to me? And do I in effect answer it by putting it through hell? Because I love it?

I'm not sure what I've done here. Maybe I've simply cheapened a myth. Shrunk a mystery down to fit my limited comprehension. Edited the divine personality until it's spookily like my own and poses no threat to my complacency.

Or maybe I've gone back where I came from. Maybe I'm home.

All I know for sure is that I'm working on it.

---

1. Mark 14:36.
2. John 20:27.

3. John 20:17.
4. Exodus 33:20.
5. Genesis 1:1–31.
6. Genesis 2:4–9.
7. Genesis 8:1.

The Three Faces of God

ANTANAS SILEIKA

PART 1 — GOD THE MONITOR

I grew up on the edge of Toronto in the fifties, in the no-man's land between the city and the country, in a working-class suburb whose religious mood resembled that of a feudal village. We may have lived in a universe that included Westinghouse, Jackie Gleason and Chrysler, but the Enlightenment was still far, far off.

My father set the religious tone in our house — kitsch Catholic, including Saint Christopher magnets for the Pontiac, a crucifix in every room and cloth scapulars for the neck. We had a variety of rosaries from the ebony beads of my father to the shine-in-the-dark variety that I laid on pillows in dark rooms, the better to impress my Protestant friends with the superiority of the one Holy, Catholic, Apostolic Church.

Although my father was a strict Catholic, his views were not entirely orthodox. He believed that one burned in hell forever for any one of a variety of infractions, from missing church on Sunday, letting meat cross one's lips on a Friday, failing to genuflect when passing before the tabernacle in Church, or disobeying one's husband.

I went to kindergarten in a Catholic convent housed in a decrepit mansion, where the black-clad nuns seemed to float noiselessly up and down the many stairs. I once arrived early on a grey winter morning to play with jig-saw puzzles. The nuns were practitioners of energy conservation, so no lamps came on before nine o'clock. I was struggling in the weak light with a devilishly difficult Three-Little-Pigs cut-out when I realized I was being watched. I looked up to see a nun standing in the corner. I was startled, but only slightly. Nuns were allied with God, and they moved in mysterious ways. For all I knew, this particular nun who watched me so attentively might have just appeared, or been there all

---

Toronto novelist and short story writer Antanas Sileika is one of sixteen authors who responded to my questionnaire concerning the spiritual aspects of the writing life. His was one of four responses I chose to reproduce in full.

night, or been standing there since the dawn of time. Like God, nuns were omniscient.

And this omniscience was terrifying, for God, like my father, had an opinion on things, and He was always ready to judge. I had no problem with the other ever-present heavenly companion, the guardian angel, for by definition the angel was gentle, like my mother. The guardian angel might sigh. The guardian angel might be disappointed, and wish I had lived up to my better self. But a guardian angel never really became cross.

God did. How angry could the Supreme Being get at a kid? Angry enough. He could get annoyed with me. He could get irritated easily, like my father when he was hung over. This God was a stickler for all the rules, the small rules. He was like the punctilious hall monitors at the elementary school I went to after kindergarten. The monitors made sure we walked silently in neat lines along the right side of the corridor; the monitors snitched on us for drinking at the water fountain when we were allowed to go to the bathroom only to accommodate the necessary bodily functions of urination and defecation, not to indulge trivial thirst.

In my child's universe, God the Monitor was everywhere. He snorted in exasperation when I climbed the branches of my neighbour's tree. He slapped a thick wooden ruler against the palms of His hands when we ate the cakes that had been stolen by more daring friends.

'Hey, you!' God shouted when we stepped on a newly seeded lawn.

'How many times do I have to tell you to close the fridge door?'

'Just look at the mud on those shoes, young man. Do you know how much new shoes cost?'

God the Monitor watched my every childhood move with the same devotion He had spent to create the world. He scrutinized me, and I felt helpless under his relentless gaze.

This nit-picking God is more or less gone now. He walked away from me one afternoon, with a dismissive wave of the hand.

The incident had to do with a very cute girl just a little younger than me. I had asked her to come behind the garage so I could examine her for early signs of polio. This very thorough examination, which later brought down on me my father's anger and my mother's disappointment, was just too much for God.

But not entirely. We were taught that there is a little bit of God in all of us, and I still see flashes of this God the Monitor from time to time. I saw Him in the eyes of the old East German border guard who stared at me long and hard at Checkpoint Charlie during the Cold War. I saw Him in the eyes of the postal clerk when I tried to re-use a franked stamp. I saw Him in my kids' eyes when they smelled traces of cigarette smoke on me.

He lurks somewhere still, exasperated, incensed, and now that I am big enough for it, occasionally enraged.

PART 2 — GOD THE STAND-UP COMIC

Unlike a lot of lapsed Catholics, I have no bitterness or anger at the Roman Catholic church. As time goes on, I am even coming to love it again. Of course, I was never hurt by my Catholicism as some others were. I look back upon my traditional Catholicism with fondness and amusement, for it was really very funny. Most religions are, but let me consider Catholicism for a moment first.

Take the rosary.

In the sixties, when everyone else was talking free love, Toronto's Exhibition Stadium was filled with thousands of Catholics clacking rosaries in their hands. It was a hot day in May, when the agnostics were tending their gardens, and their kids were swinging in parks and feeling the delicious spring air swish by their faces. But not us Catholics. We were dressed in our jackets and ties, hats and gloves for the women, and even winter coats *just in case it gets cold.* Thousands of us went to church first, or were made to go by our parents. And then we were forced to go on directly, after mass, to another religious celebration: a mass recitation of the rosary.

Of course the concession stands were closed. A hot dog or some popcorn would have been some comfort, but we were out of luck. It was one of those days when we felt cursed to have been born Catholics.

Down below us in the stadium, there were parish marching bands and banners with various saints. In the hot spring afternoon, young men fainted with some regularity as they stood to attention. We could see the collapsing standard bearers for St. Jude's and Our Lady of the Airways. Someone always stepped in to keep the satin parish banner from falling to the ground.

59

In the centre of the field stood fifty-nine girls in red dresses, all arranged in the shape of a rosary, and beside each red-dressed girl stood two others in white. As the thousands in the stands finished a Hail Mary of one of the beads of the rosary, the attending girls would fan out the skirt of the girl in red, and the giant rosary on the field blossomed before our very eyes. It was like an NFL half-time show with a religious twist.

A lot of my friends are entertained when I make jokes about Catholicism, but mine is not the only funny religion. Most religions are pretty amusing, including the new ones that don't call themselves religions at all.

First comes a loose collection that believes the whole project of Western civilization has been a sad mistake. Skyscrapers, cars, microwaves and television all came about because a few Greeks got the wrong idea. The Bible didn't help, with its 'go forth and multiply.' That instruction worked all too well, like a computer virus. These people love nature, and they will invest in Gore-tex, Kevlar, sunscreen and Chapstick to get closer to it.

Another new god has been found by my business friends. These are hard-headed types, bottom-line men who pride themselves on their shrewdness. They scorn organized religion as they do opera houses, grants to artists and socialized medicine. Then they fly off to Nevada to meet with a Zen master. Not exactly a Zen master, but the kind of guy who mixes fifteen minutes of meditation, a little personal aura identification, an afternoon with a samurai sword and an evening at a casino. These business men have found a new god, and it invariably lies within their own hearts. They really are gods themselves, these captains of finance, and need only understand it to find the power within. Now there's a joke.

I even have friends who think that health is God. They are fit-for-life vegetarians. They invited me to dinner once and served a corn and pea pie as the main course. It was repulsive. I guess the jest was on me.

The source of humour in many new spiritual beliefs lies in their fuzziness. They scorn all things traditional. They say: God is dead: May the Force be with you. Why is it easier to believe in the Force than in Yahweh? Or to put it another way, who needs new jokes when we haven't exhausted the old ones?

I come back to my Catholic roots. Most Catholics do. I have some residual fear that I am blaspheming in these reflections. I'm not so concerned about what people might think as I wonder about what goes through God's mind when He reads these words. Then I remember what the poet Czeslaw Milosz said about the old Catholic belief that one fried in hell for eternity if one missed mass on Sunday. It's a belief my father shared. Who knows, Milosz reasoned, maybe it's true. Maybe God has a sense of humour.

PART 3 — GOD THE HOLY GHOST

For most of my adult life, I have not thought much about God or religion. I imagined that I would come to them suddenly if a sober-faced doctor ever had bad news to give me. Alternatively, I would come to them eventually, as old people do. Now that I am solidly in middle age, God is beginning to show himself, elusively, in fleeting moments, like a ghost. Contrary to what Wordsworth wrote, I see more celestial light as I grow older and the mystery of it keeps growing and growing.

Take the rosary, that dear old relic of kitsch. I remember the priest preaching against its use in the early seventies, when it seemed that guitar music was more hip in church than stale old Johann Sebastian Bach. The habit of saying the rosary has pretty much died out in most places. Yet when old-time Lithuanians die, the mourning family still has the priest say a rosary at the open casket. I started going to the funerals of my parents' generation in the nineties. At one of those funerals, when I first saw the priest take out a rosary and kneel, I remembered only the intense religious boredom of my childhood. But I was a child no more.

The posture on my knees was mildly uncomfortable, and I was a little hot because I had not thought to take off my coat in that funeral home. The repetition of Hail Marys and Our Fathers put me into a kind of meditative trance. Much to my surprise, somewhere in this quiet place, behind the drone of the prayers, a strange shadow of God was flitting, faint and mysterious.

It was hard to find this God again. But one of the mysteries of God is that He comes unexpectedly, and I find traces of Him everywhere, even in my writing. I cannot pretend to be divinely inspired, but like any writer, I have sometimes found a strange kind of grace has descended upon me. There have been times when the words spilled out of me unasked, a time when the language glowed with unearthly presence, and the words seemed etched on the page to anyone who read them.

When I was young, I wanted religion to make sense. I wanted it to be good, warm, rational. I wanted God to be a socialist with a human face. He would redistribute wealth in my favour. He would be understanding of all my transgressions. He would be kind and forgiving. But who am I to dictate the characteristics of the numinous? By its very nature, the divine is divine, not human.

I know an older woman of whom I make a great deal of fun. She takes my jokes good-naturedly. She was one of the pilgrims who travelled to the religious shrine of Maggiagoria before the Yugoslav dissolution. It was said that favoured pilgrims had their rosaries turn to gold, and just such a thing happened to her. Not real gold, but gold colour. Her metal beads changed. I ridiculed her mercilessly, for this to me was a so-called sign of the worst of my childhood Catholicism. This was superstition and kitsch.

But I've come around. Who am I to say God should have good taste? Who am I to say God should be feeding the hungry instead of wasting His time changing the colours of a rosary? The divine plan, such as it is, is mysterious, unknowable, awful. The glimpses of the divine we have are partial, terrible, inspiring and frightening at the same time.

God lurks in the shadows, sometimes a friend, but sometimes other, not necessarily with the warmth and kindness I long for. His favour is a double-edged sword. He might throw me off my horse as he did Saul. He might mug me in the desert as he did Moses.

Or He might do nothing at all.

Easter Egg

Early one April I looked out onto my balcony and saw a pigeon egg. It was smaller than a chicken egg and closer to being round, but just as white.

It had no flat, crushed underside that I could see. No sticky ooze was spreading from it, either. In fact, I could almost imagine it floating over the rail with the lightness and ease of a soap bubble. Touching down without the tiniest crunch of shell.

Poised, I thought, looking at it through two slats of venetian blind. Not *sitting,* not *set* and definitely not *settled.* No, this egg was *poised* on the cement floor of my balcony. Delicately balanced on its own still-perfect curve.

I live in an old Toronto highrise where the pigeons outnumber the people. Every now and then a flyer gets pushed under my apartment door advertising a company whose mission it is to rid my building, if not the earth, of pigeons. It lists the parasites they carry, and the diseases I could get by breathing their powdered guano.

I usually just recycle the flyer, or cut it up into squares for grocery lists and phone messages. Because the fact is, I like pigeons. I've liked them from the time I first discovered they would let me walk right up to them before taking a few token flaps into the air. Even then, it was as if they were saying, 'Look. Kid. We have to do this. It's our job. Nothing personal.'

Now, as a lifelong city dweller, I respect pigeons. I admire the way they tough out the winter, thrive in the damnedest places for all the wrong reasons, take the noise and smell and danger and riches of urban living in stride. I like their stride too. Not a hop or a waddle, but an eerily human step.

So I actually felt gifted by that egg. There was something deliberate about its appearance on my balcony, I thought, as if I were being told, 'Here. See what you can do with this.'

Poised.

The word followed me around all day. Then, when I was in the middle of something, washing dishes or changing sheets, it grew into a phrase. I wrote the phrase down. Added a bit. Broke it up into lines. Looked at what I had so far.

A pigeon egg is poised
On my surprised
Cement.

So begins the one and only poem I have ever seriously tried to write. Which may be a good thing. I still have a yellowing copy of it, typed on my old electric typewriter and footnoted: Kathleen D. Miller, 1985.

According to my cv, by 1985 I had published two short stories. It was enough to make me wonder if I was turning into a real writer, but not enough to stop me worrying that my bit of success might just be a fluke. That, I've since learned, is something that never changes. After two whole books of stories, I still wonder and I still worry.

I still think about that egg, too. Once every couple of years, I take my poem out of its file and add a few words, or just rearrange the ones that are there, all the while picturing the egg out on my balcony. My present balcony, that is. I'm no longer living in the apartment I had in 1985. In fact, I've moved twice. But each time, in my imagination, the egg has managed to touch down on whatever balcony is covered by the new lease.

The poem follows me around too, though in a less mysterious way. Each time I've moved, I've simply packed it in a banker's box along with my other paper files which, with the advent of my computer, are shrinking in volume. But I'll never throw out that single sheet of paper. It's too bound up in my mind with the moveable egg for that. In fact, sometimes I get the feeling that the poem constitutes a kind of personal reckoning. As if, no matter how well I do as a writer, no matter how many books I sell or awards I win, my real success or failure will depend entirely on those few belaboured lines.

A pigeon egg is poised
On my surprised
Cement.
I watch it through the slats of blind.

That was my own take on 'through a glass darkly'. And I did watch the egg. Every now and then I'd part the venetian blinds with my fingers and take a look at it. It was oddly luminous in the cold April sunlight. And still that perfect shape.

But the days were getting warmer. At some point, unbroken or not, gift or accident, the egg would have to be dealt with in a sensible, grown-up manner.

I know what's to be done.
I have the wherewithal –
Rubber gloves and plastic bag.
I'll even hold my breath,
For, 'Lord, by now he stinketh.'
(Which sceptic, drawn to Lazarus' tomb,
Knew just what I'd be thinking?)

Stinketh. The word jumps off the tissue-thin page of the King James Version. Later translations pull the punch a bit – 'Sir, by now there will be a stench.'[1] But I like *stinketh*. It's sweaty and greasy and Jacobean.

When I first began writing my poem, I looked up the story of Lazarus in the only Bible I had at the time, a rather luridly illustrated children's edition, given to me by my grandmother when I was seven. I used to study its pictures through the interminable Sunday church services of my childhood. Actually, they were only an hour long. Presbyterians would not have stood for more. But they seemed interminable to me.

I remember being especially taken with the David and Goliath illustration, because it captured the very moment that the stone hit the giant's forehead, sending him reeling back from the tiny shepherd boy. I used to wish that Goliath's head could be tilted a little more my way, so I could see the round red hole in his skull.

As a child, I was an equal mix of morbid and innocent. Which is probably why I have such a vivid memory of being told the story of Lazarus for the first time.

It happened in grade two. I'm old enough to have attended public school when morning Bible readings were mandatory. But there was something special about this occasion. One of the school's teachers had died, and we were having a memorial service in the auditorium. A visiting minister had chosen, perhaps ill-advisedly, to read and comment on the story of Jesus raising Lazarus from the dead. When he got to the 'stinketh' part, he tried to soften the blow by adding, 'Because, as we know, when a person dies, their body begins to decay.'

Well, as a matter of fact, I *didn't* know that. I did know that people died. I even knew something about putrefaction. Some time before, I had found a dead bird in my back yard and had wanted to keep it in a shoebox in my room. A visiting great-aunt, whose generation did not believe in sweetening a child's reality, said flatly, 'It'll get all smelly and wormy if you do.' But until that minister said what he did about Lazarus, I did not make the connection that dead *people* got smelly and wormy. So for me, that day, the story of Lazarus ended not with his being brought back to life, but with his being deader than I had ever thought was possible.

Lord, by now he stinketh.

By 1985, I had left grade two far behind. But I must have been as morbidly transfixed as ever by those words, because in the next line of my poem I ask rhetorically, *Which sceptic, drawn to Lazarus' tomb, / Knew just what I'd be thinking?*

Somehow, I completely overlooked what John's gospel makes quite clear. The speaker is Martha, sister of the dead Lazarus, and in fact one of my favourite Biblical characters.

At least, she is now. Since writing the first draft of my poem, I've had time to become a little more Biblically literate. Now, I can make the connection between this Martha, who has no illusions about just how dead her brother is after four days in a hot climate, and the Martha in Luke, whose feet are planted so firmly on the ground as to be made of clay.

In the Lucan story, Jesus is a guest in the home of Martha, her sister Mary and their not-yet-dead-and-resurrected brother Lazarus. During the visit Martha emerges from the hot kitchen where she's been making everybody's lunch to demand that Jesus tell her sister to get up off her behind and come help her. Or words to that effect. Jesus answers, 'Martha, Martha, you are fretting and fussing about so many things.'[2] Then he invites her to sit down with Mary and do the one thing that is necessary, namely, listen to him.

This may be the earliest instance of someone being told to lighten up.

Though Martha's response is not recorded, I can just imagine the slow burn that starts to smoulder in her that day, then ignites much later when Jesus, having been summoned because Lazarus is sick, shows up four days after his death: 'Lord, if you had been here my brother would not have died.'[3]

I love that outburst. In a single sentence, Martha both acknowledges Jesus as divine and dismisses him as a screw-up. Then, at the tomb, her 'Lord, by now he stinketh' is another jab at him for being late.

Frankness like that takes real faith. Which may be why I avoided Martha in the first draft of my poem. Why I just didn't want to deal with her.

In 1985, I would have described myself as an accidental, or default, Christian. Though I accepted the Jesus story as one of the influences that had shaped my world-view, it would be fair to say that my Christianity was the spiritual equivalent of a shrug. Twice a year, at Christmas and Easter, I attended an Anglican mass with friends. At least part of the attraction was the opportunity to kneel and drink real wine from a common cup, actions that would have sent my Presbyterian forebears into a state of shock.

It was all very passive, and rather silly. But I see now that it was a step on a journey that I was, consciously or not, taking. My confirmation certificate is dated 1990. When the egg made its first appearance on the first of my balconies, I was just five years away from a public declaration of faith.

Pigeons come.
They bob and peer with one eye, then the other.
Bring sticks and paper, leaves and string
To lay out in a circle.
One cosies down to warm the egg,
Then flaps away,
Remembering her own.

Peeking out at the pigeons building a nest for the egg became my quiet little spectator sport. For it was undoubtedly a nest they were building, albeit after the fact. Every few minutes one of them would touch down and add something to the darkening ring of urban debris – a bit of cellophane or a scrap of tin foil. Then another would come with some crumpled Kleenex in its bill, and another with a few straws from a broom.

As each bird landed, it walked all around the egg, carefully choosing the right spot for its contribution. Murmuring to its fellows in that bubbling undertone which, as far as I'm concerned, ranks with a cat's purr as one of the two most reassuring sounds this universe has to offer.

And I found that I could, if I let myself, be tremendously reassured by the sight of the unbroken egg, its growing nest and faithful attendants. The bobbing, strutting pigeons reminded me of bosomy aunties gathered round a bassinet, naming the relatives the newborn resembled.

But there were other days when I would look out and see mourners round a coffin. And still others when all that was out there was a hunk of rotting protein whose egg-shape had triggered the nesting instinct in a bunch of birds.

> *What did that unbeliever say*
> *When Lazarus came forth blinking?*

I'll never know. Martha isn't given any lines after the fact. I do know that the next time I tinker with this poem, I'll have to at least name her, and I certainly won't be able to call her *that unbeliever.*

What *would* Martha say? She's been in mourning for four days. Now, all of a sudden, she's expected to rejoice. She has her brother back, but her hard-working, common-sense world has been turned upside down. Maybe she gives Jesus the rough edge of her tongue again. Maybe she speaks in tongues. Maybe she says nothing for the rest of her life. Maybe she goes home and makes lunch for everybody in her hot kitchen, grumbling that as usual nobody's helping her. Maybe she goes home and writes a poem.

> *What if I let out all my breath*
> *And go outside with naked hands*
> *To find a newborn,*
> *Writhing?*

I had so much trouble with those final lines. Still do. Probably always will. Maybe the problem is that I know too well what I want to say: What if I just let go of the universe as I know it, or think I know it? Open my mind up as wide as it will go for once in my life. Throw away my assumptions, my degrees, my pride. Risk making an absolute fool of myself and simply *believe*.

If a bunch of pigeons can do it, why can't I?

Every Sunday I stand up with a bunch of people and recite a creed whose assertions are every bit as preposterous as the actions of those birds: ... *The only-begotten Son of God ... Who for our salvation came down from heaven, And was incarnate by the Holy Ghost of the Virgin Mary ...*[4]

What is that? A myth? A ghost story? A tall tale? It has the earmarks of all three. Except it begins with the words, *I believe*. So what am I doing when I say those two words? Stating a fact? Making a promise? Making a wish? Telling a lie?

Frankly, at various times I've done all of the above.

Sometime between 1985 and 1990, when I changed from accidental to on-purpose Christian, I enjoyed a second childhood of faith. I believed it all – the manger scene in Bethlehem, the loaves and the fishes, the walking on water, the blind made to see and the deaf to hear, the raising of Lazarus and, yes, the resurrection of Jesus himself from the dead.

But just before my confirmation, this second childhood ended and something like a second puberty began to happen. I started picking over the gospels for the bits I could rationalize, finding fewer and fewer as Easter approached. I liked the parables for their human grittiness, and because they reveal Jesus as a storyteller, something I could identify with. And I loved the personality that shone forth from his every word and action – a radical, a poser of uncomfortable questions, a cutter through of crap.

But the miracles? Increasingly, they reminded me of parlour tricks. And the resurrection? The very underpinning of the Christian faith in all its manifestations worldwide?

At midnight on Easter Saturday, 1990, at the age of thirty-nine, I knelt before an Anglican bishop. I felt his hand on my head for about thirty seconds while he prayed aloud for me to be received into the family of the risen Christ. Minutes later, I sang with hundreds of others, *Jesus Christ is risen today ...*

And all the time, a sulky, adolescent voice inside me was saying, *Tell me another one.*

The voice pestered me more and more over the next year or so. The louder it got, the harder I tried to ignore it. Drown it out, actually, in a clamorous round of churchgoing, church-related activity and overall churchiness that I'm embarrassed now to remember.

At times, I've listened to gay friends describe the moment that they 'came out' to themselves. Stopped trying to be something they weren't and began the huge task of accepting what they were. Along with the relief of putting down the burden of deceit, there was grief for the false self that had to die – the presumed-heterosexual self who was going to live straight in a straight world. It was wrong, it was a lie, but it was like an imaginary companion that had followed them from babyhood. They were used to it. They even loved it.

My own false self was the uncritical believer, who clung to the historical, fact-based Jesus as to a teddy bear. Whose Sunday-school-level faith demanded she leave her brain in the church parking lot. Ignore the factual inaccuracies, editorial biases and self-contradictions to be found in scripture. See the Bible not as the humanly-produced bundle of documents it is, but as some kind of icon, sacred and untouchable. Forget everything she knows, as a writer of stories, about what happens to stories recorded decades after an alleged fact. How they will have lost some of their original parts and replaced them with bits of local history, ancient myth, office gossip and urban legend. How they might have exchanged one time frame or locale for another. Or coupled with older stories and begotten new ones on the way. How they will have changed, in other words, from fact to fiction.

It's so easy to be glib, now that I've come out the other end. Now that I can look back and see that I was experiencing not a loss, but a transition. Then, I felt as if I was crucifying Jesus all over again, only with no hope of resurrection.

It was a terrible feeling, and a dreadful time. The most dreadful thing about it was the way I continued to go to church, to recite the increasingly meaningless creed, to swallow bread and sip wine that had stopped being in any sense for me the body and blood of Christ.

Then one Sunday after the service I got talking to a woman who had been preparing for ordination for several years, and whose studies kept being interrupted by the birth of her children. I told her about the erosion of my belief. I tried to describe how it felt, struggled to find the right word. She found it for me.

'Scary?'

Yes. Very scary. I was afraid of trying to lead a life without a religious faith. I don't have the psychological makeup necessary for atheism. Though I have friends who are atheists, and though I respect their unbelief, I honestly don't know how they get out of bed in the morning and face yet another day in a Godless universe.

I began to wonder seriously if I should become a Jew. But I knew I couldn't. Because I was a Christian. That was, ironically, the one thing this fiasco had taught me. My heart still clung to what my mind had rejected. Though I regarded the gospels as almost pure fiction, the first six notes of 'Fairest Lord Jesus' could still bring tears to my eyes. And for the first time, I appreciated the words Mary Magdalene speaks outside Jesus' empty tomb: 'They have taken my Lord away, and I do not know where they have laid him.'[5]

Those words became a kind of mantra for me. *They have taken my Lord away, and I do not know where they have laid him.* I thought them over and over. Couldn't get beyond them. Just as, when I was a child, the story of Lazarus had ended with him rotting in his tomb, now the whole Jesus story ended with Magdalene's lament.

What if I let out all my breath
And go outside with naked hands
To find a newborn,
Writhing?

What if I cut off my head was more like it. And what exactly did I mean by those final lines, anyway? And *did* I mean it? Just how thrilled would I have been if the pigeon egg had miraculously hatched a naked, stub-winged creature that struggled toward my foot when I finally stepped out onto the balcony with my plastic bag? If I had seen its oversized beak gaping for food? Had heard its whistling, piercing shriek, telling me over and over, *I'm here! I'm here!* Felt its hard little eyes on me, bonding, imprinting?

What in fact happened was so much easier to deal with. I simply picked the egg up in rubber-gloved fingers, plopped it into a plastic bag and put the plastic bag in the kitchen garbage. There. Over and done.

There's just one problem with what in fact happened. I can't in fact remember it. Any of it. Not the gloves, not the bag, not the garbage.

But what I *can* still see, hear, almost smell, is that writhing, shrieking chick. Whenever I work on the final lines of my poem, it's out there on my balcony, waiting in fear and hunger and thirst. I know it never existed. But I gave it life with the words, *What if ...*

'*My Jesus is a fictional character ...* ' So begins an article I wrote for my church newsletter just after Easter in 1997. I had been thinking those words for a long time, had even spoken them to a few friends. But putting them in writing was still scary.

In the article I tell how, when I was struggling to believe the gospels, '*... my imagination rebelled. I let go of literalism altogether and let history blossom into story. If this sounds like a loss of faith, it was in fact the opposite. I am a fiction writer. Writing stories is how I pray. So while I have no quarrel with a Jesus who stands with feet of flesh on documented fact, for me, reading His story as fiction is the way to make it my own. And to make it real.*'

'Feed on him in thy heart by faith,' a priest says to me every Sunday, pressing a round disc of bread into my palm. Then, guiding the cup to my mouth, she says, 'Drink this in remembrance.'

Faith and remembrance. With the imagination, they form a kind of trinity. And they're all we ever have, I suppose, in the end. No matter what in fact happened.

----

1. John 11:30. Revised English Bible, Oxford and Cambridge University Press, 1989.

2. Luke 10:41.

3. John 11:21.

4. The Book of Common Prayer, General Synod of the Anglican Church of Canada (1962), 71.

5. John 20:12.

Communion[1]

My Lover, you have gotten me by heart.
If I sit or if I stand,
If I walk or if I lie,
You know it.
Across a room, across a universe,
You listen to my thoughts.
On every path I take your shadow falls,
Your footsteps echo mine.
You watch me in my bed,
And breathe my sleeping breath.
Before I speak, your silent lips
Have formed my every word.
You live in all the houses I remember,
Welcome me to houses yet unbuilt.
Your hand has learned my body's secrets
Better than my own.
Your knowledge is my terror, and my joy.
When I look away from you, I meet your knowing eyes.
When I flee, I take your hand to lead me in my flight
When I seek to hide from you, my refuge is the circle of your arms.

— Psalm 139, vv. 1–10 (somewhat reworked by K.D. Miller)

I wonder sometimes if we invent God because we're lonely. How comforting, after all, to have a divine Imaginary Companion who counts the hairs of our heads (an activity that seems to preoccupy the Judaeo-Christian God[2]), who knows our every furtive act or nasty inkling, and loves us anyway. What human relationship could possibly measure up to that?

But unconditional, limitless *anything* is beyond my limited comprehension. If I work too hard trying to picture or feel that 'love Divine, all loves excelling,'[3] I get a headache. Translating it into human terms doesn't help either, because my experiences of human love in its various manifestations are, well, human. Marked by mutual misunderstanding, irritation and boredom, with just the odd fleeting moment when it all comes together and the violins manage to play on key.

The only way I can begin to grasp the love of God, in fact, is by putting it in the context of artistic inspiration. I'm thinking of those rare times when my pen or keypad can barely keep up with an unearthly dictation I seem to be hearing. It's fair to say that I do feel loved at such times. Certainly, I feel fulfilled. Spiritually buoyed and optimistic, at least for the immediate future. But again, those moments are fleeting, and, being human, I find it difficult to sustain any belief in them during the longer stretches of writer's block.

Which may be why I feel so disaffected in church circles whenever people start talking too glibly about God's love. At times, especially if I'm blocked, the sheer repetition of the word love can be like the blows of a fist. Listening to such talk, which might as well be glossolalia, I feel as if I'm standing on the ground looking up at people who have somehow managed to sprout wings and fly. *Fly!* they call to me and each other. *Fly! Fly! Fly!* They don't know my weight. I can't imagine their lightness. They can no more feel the pressure of my feet on the ground than I can the cushion of air beneath their wings.

But in all fairness, being slightly at odds with the world, not quite 'in' with the crowd, is very much the norm for a writer. And though I don't approve of pathologizing creativity, I sometimes wonder if writers can be said to have a Pinocchio complex. We walk, we talk, but are we *real?* Do we feel what others feel or just write about it?

It has been said that in the heart of every writer is a sliver of ice that must not melt. *Must* not. In other words, it *can.* I've known two people who, in spite of enormous talent, gave up writing. Not because they were afraid of rejection or, as can sometimes be the case, afraid of success. No, they were afraid of the harm their writing might do to the people they loved.

I know that fear. The first story I ever published contained a character based on my mother. The portrait was neither cruel nor exploitive. In fact, it was a good piece of writing. But what made it good was how adroitly I had stepped outside our relationship, then looked back in with a stranger's eyes. That was my first inkling that writing was dangerous, and that being a writer was a form of psychological self-exile.

This is not to say that I don't dare fall in love, pick out sentimental birthday cards, cry at the movies or do any of the other warm, sloppy stuff that human beings do. It's just that when I write, I have to shut certain things out. Not just simple distractions like work worries or the phone or e-mail, but other things that are ingrained from babyhood. Old loyalties. Good manners. A sense of common decency that keeps me from saying the unsayable. Though they are absolutely necessary to public life, those inhibitions will melt my precious sliver of ice if I'm not vigilant. They will keep me from writing the way I must – a way that not only acknowledges but honours those furtive acts and nasty inklings that only God could love.

And I think that's what turns me off about the love of God as traditionally portrayed by the churches. There's something bourgeois and sexless about that portrayal. Baby-powder fresh. It's just too damned sweet. And it would throw up its hands in horror at the sight or smell of me the writer.

* * *

'I have had to accept that there are people in my congregation who believe I am as sinful as it is possible to be,' says a soft-spoken middle-aged woman.

'When I first came out to my parish priest,' a young man tells us, 'he advised me to try to be straight. So for three years, I did try.'

With *whom,* I can't help wondering while I listen. What a devastating bit of pastoral advice *that* was for everybody concerned.

I am sitting in a circle of people who many Christians would prefer did not exist. Or, if they must exist, would simply go away. Or, if they won't go away, would at least make an honest effort to be *normal.*

This is the annual weekend retreat undertaken by Integrity Toronto, an organization of gay and lesbian Anglicans and their friends, held each spring at the Convent of the Sisters of St. John the Divine in Willowdale, Ontario. I've been attending this retreat more or less every year since 1993, and I hate to have to miss it for any reason. It's a weekend of talking and listening to homosexuals and nuns. As a secular straight, I should stick out like a sore thumb. Yet I seldom feel more at home.

Strangeness is welcomed here, and oddity embraced. The nuns have chosen celibacy in a society that uses sex to sell mutual funds. The gays have acknowledged and affirmed their sexual orientation in a world, in a *church* no less, that is still largely homophobic. What have I done that is even remotely comparable?

Well, I'm here. Sometimes I tell people about coming here, and they give me a funny look. Someone once took me aside and asked worriedly if there were mattresses on the beds. I was tempted to answer severely that one does not require a mattress for an all-night vigil on one's knees.

As a matter of fact, the beds in the guest wing are very comfortable and the food is great. With the exception of Sunday supper, meals are eaten in silence – a rule I welcome, given my small-talk allergy. We each have our own room, named for a saint. I'm in Saint Brigid this year. The walls are pale blue, the carpet brown. There's a desk, a bed, a wardrobe, a dresser, a sink (to reduce congestion in the communal washrooms) and an easy chair. The window looks out on the garden. I can see a footpath, a bird feeder and, dimly in the distance, the glittering rush of the 401.

There is a Bible in one of the desk drawers. A small bronze crucifix is hung loosely on the wall so it can be removed and tucked out of sight, if so desired. A folded piece of cardboard on the desk reminds me of meal times in the refectory and service times in the sanctuary. I am invited, though not required, to attend any and all of the daily observances of Morning Prayer, Eucharist, Evensong and Compline.

I can spend as much time in my room as I want. I can ask for a cloth badge to wear that will announce to others that I am on silent retreat, and do not wish to speak or be spoken to. I can request, and receive, spiritual counselling from one of the Sisters.

I'm told that, at any given time of the year, CEO's and mothers account for a significant percentage of the occupants of the guest wing.

What about writers, I wonder. I write reams when I'm here, in addition to attending all services (beautifully sung by the Sisters) plus thrice-daily discussion groups with the Integrity folk. Saint Brigid, with its blue walls, is an outward and visible sign of an inward and spiritual grace – namely, a room of one's own. That grace extends to my retreat partners. No one questions or criticizes my penchant for solitude, my habit of leaving the Saturday night wine and cheese party after an hour or so. They know I go to bed early so that I can get up early, in order to write.

They have no problem with peculiarity. Besides – it was writing that got me here in the first place.

In the early nineties, my church conducted a three-part educational series on homosexuality. I was asked to write an article covering the event for *The Anglican,* the Toronto diocesan newspaper. Shortly after it was published, Chris Ambidge, the editor of *Integrator,* the newsletter of Integrity Toronto, phoned to ask if he could reprint it. He sent me some back issues of *Integrator,* and in one of them I read about an upcoming retreat. I inquired whether one had to be homosexual in order to attend. I was told no, one simply had to be human.

* * *

'My priest told me he has trouble thinking of me as quite human.'

'They are my Beloved's beloved,' one of the men answers when I ask the group how they can stand to take communion with people who hate them. As for why many of them hang in as Anglicans when MCC (Metropolitan Community Church in Toronto, serving lesbian, gay, bisexual, transgendered and heterosexual people) is available to them, one of the women reminds me that these things are not cut and dried. 'I am an Anglican,' she says. 'I was raised an Anglican. But now, to attend an Anglican service with its heterosexual assumptions and exclusive language is to do myself psychological damage. So I go to MCC. I love it there. I'm accepted, and I have friends. But I'm still an Anglican. And sometimes, I wish I could just go home.'

Many of the people in this discussion group are in a state of self-imposed spiritual exile. They did not choose their sexual orientation. But as Christians, as Anglicans, they can and do choose how closely they will continue to associate with a church that, at time of writing, after almost a decade of debate on everything from parish to Lambeth levels, and in spite of dramatic changes to the laws of this country, still sits on a homophobic fence. A church that will ordain them only if they agree to be celibate (a requirement not made of heterosexual priests.) A church that preaches tolerance of their orientation but will not bless their relationships. A church that makes a mind-boggling distinction between *being* homosexual and *doing* what a homosexual does.

At the risk of appearing to trivialize any of the above, I will say that I'm reminded of what young artists of my generation were told about how to pursue their vocation, be it writing, acting, painting or anything else. Those of us who were lucky enough not to have such nonsense ridiculed or beaten out of us were advised to marginalize it. To tuck it in around the edges of a good, sensible, paying job, or, for girls, the higher callings of wifehood and motherhood. In other words, we could be artists as long as we did not pursue our art between the hours of nine and five, or before the children were grown and gone. As long as we didn't take it *seriously*. As long as we didn't show it any real *respect*.

Sometimes I tease myself by imagining what my life would be like, what I would be like, if I had taken all the sensible, practical advice I was given while growing up. If I had majored in commerce instead of theatre. If I had never taken that leave of absence without pay to finish writing my first book. I think of the life I would be living, the person I would be, and I get scared. I don't think it's too outrageous to compare that kind of self-denial to the forced denial of one's sexual orientation − something many of the folks in this circle know all about.

In a bizarre twist of the usual scenario, I imagine 'trying' to be a lesbian, the way that young man in our group tried, on the advice of his priest, to be straight. I'm always struck by the beauty of the women in the Integrity group. Its standard is very different from the one that has goaded me at times into bouts of starvation and self-torture. I can appreciate that beauty. But could I go to bed with it? Maybe. Maybe curiosity could eclipse nature. And maybe, since I can respond as well to hand or mouth as to penis, I could reach some kind of grinding, mechanical orgasm. But the self-deception involved, not to mention the exploitation of my partner, would be as sinful as anything could possibly be.

I think the church's problem with homosexuality is, like society's reluctance to affirm and encourage young people in artistic endeavours, a symptom of something much bigger. Both, I believe, have to do with an essential joylessness. A distrust of the imagination, of the creative faculty, of sexual energy, of anything that brings laughter or pleasure or tears. It is an attitude that prevails and pervades, rendering even the love of God parochial and conditional and prudish.

If I go by what I've most often felt in churches throughout my life, I will have to believe that God loves the portion of me that exists from the waist up and the chin down. Well, I happen to think there's more to God than a tit man. And I have Integrity to thank for helping me keep the faith.

These retreats provide me with an opportunity to talk about my spiritual and my sexual selves in the same breath. It was during one of them that I said out loud what I had been almost afraid to think – that for me the Eucharist can be an erotic experience. Well, why not? Every Sunday I hear a (usually) male voice say on behalf of the Son of Man, 'This is my body....' And then I take that Body into my own. Being able to voice such thoughts in a tolerant, unshockable, *religious* setting led to my being able to write them down in the short story 'Requiem' which appears in my first book.

·At these retreats, through getting to know some of the Sisters, I have come to a new understanding of celibacy as a positive and creative state. Like many people living in a sex-obsessed society, I had assumed there was something pathetic about nuns – that they were fearful, prudish creatures in flight from reality. Now, I have so much respect for these women – for their intelligence and strength and humour. One of them, Sister Thelma-Anne, our retreat leader, has this to say about the most misunderstood of her vows:

Celibacy is more than just abstinence. It is a call and a way of life. ... There is something highly intentional about celibacy. ... [It] is a response to God's gift of sexuality, a way of releasing its creative and generative energy to further God's reign, to love without the need to possess, and to reach out beyond oneself to embrace all humanity. ... I can love deeply as a celibate. Being in touch with my sexuality is essential to my life of prayer. When I fall into desolation, routine or rebelliousness, it is usually because I have slipped back into the heresy that I am a disembodied mind and that my body is a nuisance, an unpleasant reminder of needs and urges I would sooner forget. In this sort of denial, the casualties are not just prayer and a sense of God's presence, but also creativity, joie-de-vivre, compassion, flexibility, and the capacity to respond to beauty. This is not surprising; our spirituality and our sexuality flow from the same source, the deep well-spring of God's creative love within us.'[4]

It took me a long time to appreciate what 'T.A.' is saying here. I finally realized that I needed to 'come out' to myself, proudly, as a celibate. Because I have been one, for the last seven or so years. I didn't choose to live without sex, and at first my 'not getting any' was a source of panic and shame. Then I learned to joke about it, ruefully and self-deprecatingly. But in the last year or so, I've caught myself *liking* it. There is a marked lessening of stress in my life that comes of finding intimacy in friendship alone. I have a deep sense of peace and self-containment that nourishes me both spiritually and creatively. And I don't think it's at all accidental that this development in my life roughly coincides with two others – acknowledging and exploring my religious faith, and publishing my three books. They are all thickly intertwined, I am sure, though in ways that it might take me a fourth book to understand.

* * *

The feeling I get from these Integrity retreats is one of being 'all present and accounted for'. My existence has tended to be fragmented and compartmentalized. I've erected a psychological barrier between my writing career and my day job. None of my lovers was ever a man of faith. Only a few of my friends and colleagues are comfortable hearing about the spiritual side of my life. Even in my parish church, I still feel obliged to discipline my sense of humour, launder my language and leave my sexuality at the door. But for some reason, I manage to get it all together when I'm part of a group of people with whom many would say I have nothing in common.

I started this essay by lamenting that I have trouble experiencing the love of God in religious settings. There was, however, one time when something managed to shine through. Not surprisingly, it happened during an Integrity retreat – my first, in fact.

It was Sunday morning. We had stripped our beds as requested, and put our used towels in the marked bins in the hall of the guest wing. We had packed and arranged for rides home and asked one of the Sisters to take a picture of us all in the small chapel where we have our discussions. 'I don't think it's going to come out straight,' she said afterwards, then joined in our laughter.

We filed into the sanctuary for a final service of Communion. We waited for the visiting priest to arrive. And waited. Through some

COMMUNION

scheduling glitch, he or she didn't show. Canonical law forbids lay people to bless, break and offer the Body of Christ, so after a hasty Morning Prayer service, we trooped out of the sanctuary and back into the chapel. We had nothing to stay for, but didn't want to leave. There was such a feeling of incompleteness in the air.

I don't remember whose idea it was. Or whether the bread was from the sanctuary or the refectory. Maybe the wine was consecrated, and maybe it was left over from the party the night before. One of the women read the Eucharistic prayer. We sat in our usual circle and served each other. The man to my right tore off a bit of bread and handed it to me. 'Kathleen,' he said. 'Our new sister. The Body of Christ. The bread of heaven.' Then it was my turn to serve the woman on my left. I fumbled with the bread. Stumbled over the words. And managed not to cry.

---

1. This essay is based in part on articles I have published in *Integrator*, which is the newsletter of *Integrity*, Toronto.

2. Matthew 10:29–30.

3. From the eighteenth-century hymn by Charles Wesley.

4. From 'Ways of Prayer and Celibacy' by Sister Thelma-Anne ssjd, published in *Integrator* (1998), issue no. 2.

An Amazed Witnessing

Early in January 2000 I sent a three-page questionnaire to twenty authors whose work has been published by The Porcupine's Quill. I asked them about their religious background, their present belief or unbelief in a deity, their writing rituals, what they thought about inspiration, why they needed to go on writing and whether society would suffer if they stopped.

As the replies started coming in by snail and e-mail, I saw that what was happening was a quiet conference of the written word. Nobody travelled, booked into a hotel or took part in a panel discussion. But the responses echoed each other so clearly and so often that at times I wondered if something telepathic was going on.

Four of the sixteen authors who responded did so in the form of discrete personal essays I preferred to reproduce in full, and which appear elsewhere in this book. Each comes from a different religious tradition, and is at a different stage of their career. The common ground, for them and for the other twelve, is of course writing. As for religion, Toronto poet and short story writer Mike Barnes speaks for the majority when he confesses that: 'thinking about spiritual matters makes me feel an all-over itch, one I can't scratch.'

* * *

So why send out a questionnaire? Officially, to gain some perspective. As I said in my cover letter, 'When I first started writing about the link between creativity and spirituality, I assumed I could get by with picking my own brain. Several essays later, the pickings are getting rather slim. So I'm asking for some help from my Porcupine's Quill colleagues.'

That was true enough, and it was indeed refreshing to deal with thoughts and opinions other than my own. But I suspect the real reason for reaching out lay a little further beneath the surface.

A popular Christmas carol begins, 'Do you see what I see?' I almost used that line as the title of this essay. The title I did choose, 'An Amazed Witnessing', is taken from one of the writers' responses, and strikes closer to the heart of the matter. Frankly, I wanted witnesses. Whether they confirmed or refuted my testimony didn't matter. I just wanted to feel that I was not alone in turning and looking in this particular direction at this particular time.

But what did I mean by 'my testimony?' Good question. Because my pew was getting comfortable. A decade of regular, institutionalized worship had dulled the hunger that led me back to church in the first place. So I knew I needed to be challenged.

And I was.

* * *

Perhaps the most objective, even somewhat scientific, response to the questionnaire came from Toronto short story writer Gil Adamson, whose church-going grandparents 'laughed if you asked them if they believed in God' and whose father 'was a full-out enemy of Religion'. She remembers the one time her father did take her to church, 'where we sat at the back, and Dad kept a quiet, Socratic-method lesson going, most of which translated into: that man up there is lying to you, Gil'. Interestingly enough, both she and her brother studied the anthropology of religion in university. 'I guess that's where I come from,' she writes. 'Bible as literature, religion as sociological phenomenon. Religion as crowd control, or, in the desert, as a means of ensuring cleanliness and safety.' Still, she admits, 'I have intermittently tried – harder than most people, I believe – to "sense" a God, Judaeo-Christian or otherwise. I have tried to imagine an afterlife. I'm afraid I agree with my great-grandmother: "after this, there's nothing." It's hard to overstate how much that worries me.'

That note of wistful unbelief, which I heard in more than one of the responses, made me wonder whether there are *theistic* and *atheistic* personalities – people who by nature want to believe 'in something' and will at least try to do so, and others who are actively repelled by the prospect.

With regard to the latter, I was privileged to hear from Toronto novelist and self-described 'old fashioned rationalist mechanist atheist' Russell Smith, whose submission was without doubt the most passionate of the sixteen. 'I am evangelical in my anti-spiritualism,' he declares. 'I am hostile not just to organized religion, but to any form of spiritual belief, organized or non, to jihad-waging institutions and to yoga-inspired meditations alike, to any talk of spirit or chakras or life-force or gods or fairies or elves.... I am afraid of anybody who says he or she believes in any alternate plane of reality, that is, any plane of reality that is not what we experience daily. This includes the ideas of spirit, of god and of afterlife, and so includes all religions, including the non-violent ones like Taoism or Baha'i. I am afraid of these people because they can always retreat into that belief as an answer to rational argument.'

Well, I don't actually think I would scare Russell much if I bumped into him on my way to church. But I am grateful to him for his honesty, and for squelching the last niggling doubt I might have had that the topic I'm dealing with here is a hot one.

* * *

'I feel about religion as I feel about goodness: attracted and deeply distrustful.' This assertion by Ottawa novelist Elizabeth Hay captures the ambivalence expressed by almost all the writers when answering questions about the faith of their fathers. 'I was a thoughtful little boy,' reflects Montreal author Ray Smith, 'and went to United Church of Canada Sunday school and church until I left home the day after the graduation ball in 1963.... My children are also thoughtful little boys and should, I think, have at least some sense of the Christian heritage of our civilization. I have considered taking them to church, but the new [United Church] Hymnal, with its John Denver, Karen Carpenter, Rod McKuen sentiments, is repulsive.... I'm not sure what to do; not surprising for an agnostic.' This need for something that organized religion doesn't seem to offer was expressed by a number of respondees, including Stratford author Marianne Brandis, who admits: 'I sometimes have a hankering towards a spiritual dimension which, so far as I can see, has nothing to do with going to church.'

For many, the disenchantment with established faiths set in early. Ottawa short story writer Mary Borsky remembers thinking during a church service, 'Okay, I can believe in God, but I can also believe in anything. For example, I can believe that right now there's a turnip beside the door. And I would grow so convinced of the turnip's existence, that I was compelled to turn around to see whether it was really there or not.' Toronto's Carol Malyon, who has written for children as well as adults, dreamed as a youngster of being a missionary, and attended church three times per Sunday: '... to the United Church in the morning, to bible class in the afternoon, then to an Anglican service at night because the darkness and rituals and tidbits of Latin seemed more church-like.' But the walls of the institution could not contain her growing intellect: 'Once I started to question, it took a while but essentially the whole thing was over.'

Even the lone practising Catholic in the group, *Toronto Star* book columnist Philip Marchand, had a temporary Damascus-in-reverse experience: 'I can recall one moment as an undergraduate walking on the path in the University College quadrangle when I thought, with a kind of bitter exultation, yes, I *am* an atheist. Marx and Sartre were right.' Now, though he attends mass every week and prays daily, he still has '... immense trouble imagining the Deity as personal. It's easier to believe in a kind of Life Force, or even Buddhist vacuum – although, as Wyndham Lewis points out ... the Life Force is always a blind organism, and I can't accept that God is blind.'

He was anything but, remembers Toronto novelist Cynthia Holz. And He had no trouble at all getting personal. 'I carried a strong image of a watchful, censorious God in my mind throughout my girlhood,' she writes. 'This God seemed especially upset by the fact that I was a frequent masturbator and often appeared at inappropriate times to wave an accusatory finger at me.' Holz, who was taken to synagogue as a girl and whose mother admonished, 'Don't question religion!' ended up doing just that. Her rewriting of the God of her childhood began when she was expelled at the age of eleven from Hebrew school for 'having a fresh mouth'. Later, in her teens, '... I began to follow my own path and to decide, among other things, that holiness had little to do with arcane rituals and more to do with personal traits and how you treated others. Empathy, sensitivity, self-awareness, perceptiveness: these became my code words for true spirituality – and, coincidentally, happened to be good qualities for a would-be writer to develop.' Now, she says, 'I think of myself as an agnostic, yet freely invoke the name of God in times of stress and fear. This is not the severe, punitive God of my childhood but a benign, amorphous spirit who patiently hears my pleas even if I get no response.'

Leaving one's childhood house of worship to seek a God of one's own was the pattern for most of the respondees, making them part of a rapidly growing population of what I will call, at the risk of sounding presumptuous, the spiritually homeless. Not that they are in any way pathetic souls. Far from it. The pathos lies in the religious roofs that tried to shelter them and the dogmatic walls that tried to contain them.

But even if their leave-taking was relatively amiable, as it was for Mike Barnes, who attended Anglican services into his twenties, it did leave its mark. 'I couldn't say I believe in God,' admits Barnes, 'but I am not an unbeliever either.... On that paradox, or ambiguity, I'm pinned and wriggling.' As for what might tempt him back inside a house of worship: '... a god, a power, a faith, would by definition have to be at least as large as I am ... so if I have to leave elements of myself at the door, it's ipso facto bogus – throw off ballast of sex, humour, paradox, tragedy, doubt, reason, magic? – lose any of these and you're fucked at the starting gate.'

* * *

Of course, you don't have to be a writer to have your intelligence insulted, your imagination pinched or your sexuality politely ignored by organized religion. But there is a side of communal worship that seems to be especially irksome to authors, and that is its very communalism. Marianne Brandis puts her finger on what may keep many away from groups and gatherings, religious or otherwise: 'My main problem is that I'm not a joiner, and Sunday mornings are prime writing time.'

Not a joiner. Institutionalized fellowship, the social side of regular worship, incurred such widespread dislike that I began to wonder if hermitry might be the true religion of writers. Elizabeth Hay, a non-practising birthright Quaker, asserts, 'The trouble with Quakers is twofold: there's no music, and they're too nice.... You can't go to a Quaker meeting without shaking everybody's hands afterwards. Supposedly the most direct form of communion with God, unmediated by a minister, it makes you most aware of the people around you, whose stomachs grumble as embarrassingly as your own, and who feel "moved" to speak.' Though she tempers her criticism with admiration for the way Quakers 'take in all sorts of strays ... oppose war and injustice [and] don't mind being unpopular,' for Hay the bottom line is that religion at its best 'offers the exquisite pleasures of music and *solitude* [Italics mine].'

But the impulse to be alone is more than an allergic reaction to the madding crowd. Solitude is writing's medium. It is actively sought and rigorously defended. Carol Malyon even suspects that she moves around a lot not just to find new settings for characters and their stories, but also '... so I can remain an outsider, keep the distance I need, that vague sense of isolation and unease, in order to write.'

More than one of the respondees spoke of the public side of a writer's life – interviews, readings, book-signings – as a necessary evil. 'The post-publication nonsense,' states Gil Adamson, 'fills me with mortification and regret. That is not an overstatement. Luckily, I don't think less of the work ... I just think less of myself.' Kingston novelist, poet and short story writer Steven Heighton agrees that the unavoidable publicizing and selling of the finished product is a disruption of the necessarily solitary process: '... the glib argot of the wine and cheese party or the stereotyped patter of the interview or the prating of the ego, in those fleeting times when you begin to credit the hyperbole of your best reviews, are all forms of dead language. I doubt I'm the only writer who has found that when the readings are over it can take a while to tune in again to the right inner station and get back to writing in a clear voice.'[1] He goes so far as to recommend '... a kind of controlled agoraphobia' for writers, to enable them '... to return, in silence and privacy, to the true self. And to the authentic things it has to say.'

Silence and privacy. The very things corporate worship puts out of reach of the worshipper. I must say that I felt personally vindicated by what my colleagues had to say about their need to keep the world at a slight remove. As a member of a church congregation, I have sometimes guilted myself out for not being more involved, for not dropping in more often to Coffee Hour, for ceasing all committee work in recent years, and for having distinctly uncharitable thoughts about pew mates who chatter during the service. So I greatly appreciated Mary Borsky's honesty when she admitted 'coming to experience the Christian imperative to love as oppressive'.

Not that I can reasonably object to the two main commandments of my religion, which are to love God and love my neighbour. (Especially since, as I once heard spelled out in a sermon, I am not compelled to *like* my neighbour.) But some Christian denominations, in my opinion, have cheapened both the word and the concept, turning the love of God into something sweet and automatic, like Divine Pez.

When I was shopping for a denomination, Anglicanism appealed to me because the service is calm and beautiful, and gives a person some breathing space. I'm not as apoplectic as some Anglicans about the passing of the Peace, which involves, at a set time in the service, turning to one's pew mates, shaking hands and saying, 'The peace of Christ', or, 'Peace be with you'. On the other hand, I could definitely live without it. Even that small ceremony can feel arbitrary and forced, like an unwanted embrace.

That's another side of organized religion that probably turns off many a writer. Any worship service, regardless of the faith involved, is essentially a *made thing*. And it might be safe to say that writers, generally speaking, prefer to stay home and make their *own* thing. I couldn't help remarking that, of the thirteen respondees who admitted to a belief in some kind of spiritual reality, only four – a Jew, a Catholic, a Buddhist and a Native spiritualist – regularly set aside time for religious observance. And even they confess to being less than orthodox. As for me, although I'm in church most Sunday mornings, my reciting of the Nicene Creed is becoming an act of almost pure hypocrisy as my own designer faith increasingly resembles agnosticism with a spritz of Jesus.

This state of affairs is probably not peculiar to writers. It may be the case with any intelligent individual who wants to believe in something above and beyond the quotidian, but has yet to find an established religion that is not Procrustean in effect. If such an individual does join a faith community, it is more likely the faith itself that gets stretched or cropped to fit.

* * *

So what is the 'religious experience' of the writer? Is there a 'faith community' that would make this necessarily solitary soul feel welcome? According to the responses, it would have to be one that, like the faith itself, is essentially home-made.

Speaking of her friends, children and grandchildren, Carol Malyon claims, 'These folks and my writing are so important that I can't use a metaphor strong enough to express it. Bedrock, maybe.' Even the very act of writing, while requiring solitude, can be a way of reaching out to a kind of community, a family of sorts. In her chapbook *Singularity,* Mari-anne Brandis muses, 'For me, lacking posterity, having little family, what gives meaning to life? Writing does, not only the final product but the creative process itself, the constant research and thinking, and then the shaping and crafting. The books I write, and the connections they make with readers, are vitally important to me. I'd *much* rather have readers than children and grandchildren.'[2]

Connection was a word that came up again and again in the responses. Connection with self, with readers, with other artists and with what Oakville poet and former Contact Press editor Peter Miller calls 'a plane apart'. Miller, whose spiritual journey has spanned Chris-tian Science, Transcendental Meditation and Buddhism, recalls artistic experiences which 'now seem to me to resemble meditation: a kind of ecstasy, or what religion calls atonement (at-one-ment): arising for example from Margot Fonteyn dancing in Swan Lake, certain paintings or sculptures, some writings. Such were my reading of Rilke's Tenth Duino elegy, in my unseasoned German, while strolling through New York's Central Park; drowning in the thrills of John Le Carré's *Smiley's People* and *The Honourable Schoolboy;* and at many other times savour-ing strong literature. Those occasions enter my world of spirituality because they have for the moment extracted my ego and have at-one-d it with the wizardry of other people's creations.'

The strongest case for a direct link between creativity and spirituality was made by Steven Heighton, who writes, 'Art began as religion and art is still religious, always – even the most "secular" art, the most scatolog-ical, profane, the most rational or "anti-religious" – because art in its own way is always tied up with the staple questions, the elemental mysteries that all religions start with and always struggle to explore and explain. And of all the arts, literature is the one most intimately linked to religion – "religion" not as specific creed, or institution, but as all-embracing perspective. This world-perspective is one I think of as uni-tive, inclusive, and connectional....'

Mary Borsky, however, sees a more tenuous link between the two. 'I can't really relate writing to religion at this point in my life, though I think at one point I did feel the conjunction of the two, mostly, I think, in a quiet witnessing of the world, an amazed witnessing. Something like that. I welcome arriving at that place again.'

Not so Russell Smith: '…I hope you are not going to argue that all writers, because they rely on a heightened sensitivity and on important rituals, are participating in some kind of spiritual reality,' he warns. 'Count me out. All of my heightened states – even the trance-like state one gets into while visualizing a scene or writing dialogue – can be explained without recourse to spirits and fairies and elves.'

What, then, is inspiration?

Questions about where ideas come from and whether the writer is always in control of the work elicited the widest range of opinion from the respondees. On the one hand, there was Philip Marchand's 'It is not unthinkable that the Holy Spirit might play a role sometimes in artistic inspiration.' On the other hand, there was Russell Smith's 'I am in total control of my ideas.' In between, there were several who were willing to concede that there are times in their writing lives when something at least a little spooky is going on.

'Inspiration,' writes Peter Miller, 'starts with a *compulsion* to compose on a particular subject, and continues with a *recognition* that in the process one has hit upon the absolute word or phrase (or melody, or design) which is a serendipitous discovery from one's own depths that yet harmonizes with outside truths. One is in control of it if one gives free rein to the inspiration's scope without spoiling it by an excessive effort to correct humanly what is innately divine…. Inspiration is certainly a kissing-cousin to mysticism, and a creative artist at the best is a mystic.'

Mike Barnes agrees that at times something besides his conscious, controlling self seems to be toiling away at his desk. 'I can choose to write, but I can't choose to write well; the latter chooses me … I was forced into this realization because only the stories that took me by storm, that I felt I had no choice but to write, attained real vitality … all the rest, no matter how diligently or devoutly or resourcefully or continually I worked at them, failed.'

Nevertheless, a wide practical streak did reveal itself in many of the respondees' attitudes to inspiration. Ray Smith writes, 'As for God, Angels, Muses, or divine Inspiration in my writing, I'm perfectly happy to welcome them, but I've always found it best while I'm waiting to trust not to inspiration, but to perspiration. I do think I have three times experienced the power of the work to take over my life, if that has anything to do with inspiration. While writing "Serenissima" (my best short story) and the two sections of "The Continental" (a two-part novella, and my finest writing) I was teaching a brutal five-course load, doing an MA in the evenings from Concordia, spending nine hours a week pumping iron and running, and doing much of the cooking at home. Yet I would find myself drawn to the typewriter at eleven at night; I'd work until one or two, then sack out. Only to have the material call to me at four or five; I'd get up and work until seven or eight. So it went on for weeks, months. Is that the Divine Breath?'

Whatever it is, it comes and goes in the life of the writer. 'There are days when I feel "inspired" and write several pages in one sitting,' admits Cynthia Holz, 'but I never wait for those times. Daily, dogged effort is required to finish a project, and I am content to write as little as one page if it's a good one. For me, inspiration is a confluence of high energy, original thoughts and intense focus that comes from inner stillness or perhaps some hormonal rush – those times when the world falls away and nothing matters but the words in my head and the ones on the page. I cannot make these times happen, but I am aware of them and quick to take advantage of them when they occur.'

Holy Spirit or human sweat? Elizabeth Hay admits to being downright superstitious about the whole thing. 'I seem to have a rather strong belief in the evil eye. That's why I don't speak about writing in terms of inspiration, but in terms of work. Boasting about inspiration, it seems to me, is asking for big trouble.'

Steven Heighton agrees that whatever it may be, inspiration has a mind of its own and will be neither summoned nor controlled: '... those rare best poems and stories are the ones that seem to hunt us down.... Inspiration is a form of ambush.'

* * *

Several years ago, a friend described for me the effect my writing had on her. She said that what I did was take some commonplace thing – a brush with a few hairs in it, for example, or a hand resting on a cane – and *turn* it. Just *turn* it a few degrees one way or another so that she was looking at it from a new and different angle.

Well, I wasn't aware of doing any turning. As far as I was concerned, I was trying to get down on paper, in the clearest possible language, exactly what I perceived. So I had to conclude that the strange angle from which I caused my friend to see things was, for me, the norm. In other words, I suffered from a kind of creative visual impairment.

Not that I want to pathologize the work of the artist. There are probably mental-health professionals out there who would happily render Michelangelo a well-adjusted shoe salesman if they could, instead of someone who felt compelled to paint that silly ceiling. I confess to being irritated by the sand-in-the-oyster theory, too, or any other that tries to rationalize artistic creation. The desire and ability involved are not some kind of problem or sickness that in a perfect world would be solved, cured, exorcized or amputated. I don't write because there's something wrong with me. I write because I'm a writer.

Now, my own personal spin on all this is that I believe God made me a writer, and delights when I answer that call. I have no theology to back me up here. All I've got is a hunch, based on the fact that I feel great when I write and lousy when for any length of time I don't.

St. John of the Cross coined the phrase 'dark night of the soul'. Whenever I come across his description of that spiritual state, I'm struck by how much it sounds like writer's block. And when I asked my colleagues if they needed, as well as wanted, to write, and what the consequences were of that need not being met, their responses put me in mind of the Psalms.

Mike Barnes: '[Writing] is sacred to me, yes, and necessary like oxygen ... in the wordless periods, which are unfortunately legion, part of me shrivels and dries up.'

Cynthia Holz: 'Yes, I need to write.... Writing involves my whole self, both conscious and unconscious, intellectual and emotional, and satisfies me as no other task can.... When I'm not writing it's usually because I'm busy doing other things ... but a steady diet of other work leaves me feeling restless and discontent, pining to start scribbling again.'

Peter Miller: 'I need, as well as want, to write. It is an urge towards self-expression. Without it, there is a drastic lack of fulfilment, quite comparable to deprivation of sex. At worst comes the doubt whether there is any self to express.'

Carol Malyon: 'Of course I need to write. Absolutely. Otherwise why in the world would I spend my time this way? People manage to lead perfectly happy fulfilled lives without writing. Society will not realize it is impoverished if it doesn't receive my stories. But I'm the only one who can tell my version of the world. I have to do it. If I don't tell it, it will never be known. I am very edgy when I'm kept from writing for very long. But that's right now. Will a time ever come when I feel I've said all I need to say? Somehow I doubt it. I believe with John Gardner that one keeps trying to tell a story, always the same one, and not quite doing it, so keeps having to begin all over again.'

Society will not realize it is impoverished if it doesn't receive my stories. That sad conviction marked many of the responses to the questions, 'Do you believe our society needs for you to go on writing? What are the consequences of that need not being met?' Again, an image of spiritual homelessness arose – of writers with no fixed address in an increasingly post-literate society where fewer and fewer readers have the time or the inclination to linger lovingly over a single phrase.

But even if they share that bleak vision, writers do go on writing, if only for the sake of giving back at least as much as they have taken. Speaking of how she and everyone who reads has a personal canon of favourite authors, Gil Adamson muses, 'Who knows if they made the world better? But imagine erasing them, taking away what you learned from reading their books. Doesn't the world seem smaller?'

Indeed it does, agrees Marianne Brandis. 'I know how other writers' books have shaped and enriched my life,' she writes. 'I have an obstinate faith that mine can do the same for others.'[3]

That 'obstinate faith' is what keeps Mike Barnes at his desk. 'I believe that writing is a non-entropic force, something that can yield more energy than went into making it … and the world needs all the non-entropy it can get … I believe the world would, in some unmeasurable way, be a slightly less excellent place without my effort.' Then he adds, too modestly, 'My effort more than my result.'

---

1. All Steven Heighton quotations are taken from his essay, 'Still Possible to Be Haunted,' from *The Admen Move on Lhasa* (Anansi, 1997), which he sent me as a very apt response to my questionnaire.

2. Brandis, Marianne, *Singularity* (2000), 12.

3. Ibid. p. 12.

No Coward Soul

No coward soul is mine
No trembler in the world's storm-troubled sphere
I see heaven's glories shine
And Faith stands equal arming me from Fear [1]

In the year or two before Emily Brontë wrote those lines, she was part of a household whose storm-troubled sphere might have been designed to drive her insane.

Her sister Charlotte, who had yet to put the names Jane and Eyre together, was pining for a French professor who had essentially told her to leave him alone. An understandable rebuff, given the kind of thing he (not to mention his wife) was likely to find in the letters his former pupil addressed to him: '... when day by day ... the sweet delight of seeing your handwriting and reading your counsel escapes me as a vision that is vain, then fever claims me – I lose appetite and sleep – I pine away.' [2]

Meanwhile in the same house, Emily's brother Branwell was telling the world that his latest in a series of firings came of his being the innocent object of his boss's wife's infatuation: '... Three months since I received a furious letter from my employer, threatening to shoot me if I returned from my vacation....' [3] Branwell had in fact made the story up out of whole cloth, yet believed it more fervently with every telling.

'What a blessed relief it must have been for Emily,' writes Daphne du Maurier, 'to stride away over the moors with her dog, and put aside, if only for an hour on a winter's afternoon, the memory of her brother humped on his bed thinking of his Lydia, and her sister crouched on the dining-room sofa brooding on her professor.' [4]

Blessed relief indeed. I can even see her rounding on the parsonage from a distance, practically spitting a prototype *No Coward Soul* at the house and its self-absorbed inhabitants:

Vain are the thousand creeds
That move men's hearts, unutterably vain,

Worthless as withered weeds
Or idlest froth amid the boundless main
To waken doubt in one
Holding so fast by thy infinity
So surely anchored on
The steadfast rock of Immortality

Not exactly someone to tell your troubles to.

I have no wish to trivialize the poem, or to ignore its essentially religious nature. But even the most transcendent work comes of the stuff of someone's life, and bears the marks of their personality.

The author of *No Coward Soul* brooks no nonsense and suffers no fools. Her faith is pared to the bone, comfortless and uncompromising, equipped with neither fairest Lord Jesus nor tender Mother Mary to buffer the believer from her God. Across a moor, across an ocean, through time and whatever separates the dead from the living, it aims one barb after another at cowardly, trembling, vain, worthless, withered, idle souls everywhere.

My own included.

* * *

I'm intensely curious about the particulars of any author's life. I want to know what they ate and who they loved and whether they wrote sitting at a kitchen table or perched up in a tree. There is comfort in such details, I've found, and reassurance. Reading about the frustrations, false starts and disappointments experienced by other writers puts my own in perspective. The same goes for their joys and accomplishments and bits of good luck. I suppose, in a way, I'm looking for company.

Not that I want to add my voice to that popular chorus of moans about the 'loneliness' of the writing life. Writers in fact relish the chance to be alone, and guard it fiercely. So when I say that I read literary biographies as a way of looking for company, I mean a sort of spiritual communion. A validation through association.

Though I've published three books, I still hesitate mentally to apply the words *writer* and *author* to myself. It's not that I think I'm a fraud. It's just that writing is such an ongoing process. At no point can I pass an exam or frame a certificate that will proclaim me a bona fide 'writer'.

Publication does help, but not as much as might be supposed. I published my first short story as the result of winning a literary contest – a double whammy that left me paralysed, unable to write for a full year. Whenever I tried, I felt as if I was suddenly performing on stage in blinding light something I had previously done furtively in the dark. What finally freed me, oddly enough, was the news that a second story of mine had been accepted for publication. With that, the extraordinary became just a little bit ordinary. My eyes, so to speak, adjusted to the light.

But there is always some tension between the private and public sides of a writer's life. Again, a writer's solitude is a writer's treasure, one that must be guarded and protected from a world that will snatch it away if it can. So when the world suddenly comes knocking, wanting a bio, a photograph, maybe an interview, it's very hard to let those defences down.

Except for what we can infer from their work or winkle out of their associates, all we know of a writer's private life is what they surrender, willingly or not, to the public. In Emily Brontë's case, the struggle between private and public was quite literally a fight to the death. Her sisters had to practically drag her out of obscurity. She begrudged the very fact of publication, barely co-operated in its processes and refused to meet her publishers. She died unwillingly famous at the age of thirty, indifferent to the hostility generated by *Wuthering Heights*, and giving every sign of wishing the world had simply left her alone.

Which of course it won't do. When it comes to Emily Brontë, I'm as fascinated as I ever am by her day-to-day existence and the secrets of her writing life. I want the same validation from her that I seek from any author. I can even name a few very basic things she and I have in common. We're both women, both writers, and both, in our albeit different ways, religious. What is more, when I read *No Coward Soul*, I can feel some of her personal vindication, the fierce, angry joy that points each flinty word.

But that's as close as I can get without paying a price. More like a tithe, actually. I'm composing this essay during the season of Lent; and though I didn't intend it to, the exercise is starting to resemble a penitential rite.

There is something chastening about Emily Brontë. She sets an example that reproaches as much as it inspires. And I have a feeling that getting to know her better will mean venturing onto dangerous ground.

Because holy ground is always dangerous.

* * *

There is a portrait of the Brontë sisters painted by their brother. In it, Charlotte and Anne gaze sweetly, even romantically, into middle distance. They are as posed and composed as any proper young ladies of their day.

Then there's Emily. She all but glares straight at the viewer. Her expression is one that might greet some trembling, coward soul who dared enter her unheated room in the Haworth parsonage, causing her to look up from her rosewood writing desk. Her jaw is clenched, her lower lip thrust out, and her eyes as cold as the question they appear to ask: *Just exactly what is your business with me?*

All right, what is my business with Emily Brontë? As a writer, why am I most intrigued by the least prolific of the three sisters – the one who left behind a handful of poems and a single novel? Even Anne, who lived just a few months longer than Emily, produced twice as much; and Charlotte, of course, went on to earn her living as a novelist.

twice as much ... earn her living ... As if numbers of words and amounts of money were the measure of anything, when it comes to literature. Still, I did wax quantitative there, didn't I? Nor would I exactly turn my nose up at the royalties from a string of best-sellers.

Yes, things have changed. For better or worse, I seem to have gotten over my initial deer-in-the-headlights reaction to publication. Now, I'll travel any distance to read for half an hour to a small audience in return for a slim honorarium, and never begrudge the time or effort. During interviews, I burble away nonstop. At book signings and literary festivals, I've been known to all but grab the lapels of passersby and treat them to an in-your-face sales pitch that leaves them stumbling away, clutching one of my books in a low state of shock.

At home, I court oblivion by keeping multiple copies of all my reviews, good and bad, clipped together in handy press-release-style packets. I never send a letter without making a copy, and store all letters received in carefully labelled files. And yes, Reader, I *do* keep a diary, lest, God forbid, my future biographers be in the slightest doubt as to how I spent my days.

In my first book, the character Raymond Mayhugh confesses:

I've always had a dim picture in the back of my mind of quiet, slow-moving people going through my effects. 'These were the poems he admired,' they say, peeking into my file marked Poems. 'These were his thoughts,' they murmur, reading my diaries. And leafing through my scrapbooks, they intone, 'This was his life.'

I have spent my life laying myself out for burial. I have become my own memorial, my own museum.[5]

It's fear, of course. Not so much fear of physical death as fear of sinking without a ripple; of being that hypothetical tree whose falling in the forest makes no sound because nobody hears it. It may be the biggest, darkest fear of all – ceasing to exist even in memory, being present in the mind of no one.

But this is, again, the season of Lent. And doesn't my religion teach me that I *am* present in the mind of God, even after death? And shouldn't that be enough for me?

Though Earth and moon were gone
And suns and universes ceased to be
And thou wert left alone
Every Existence would exist in thee

In spiritual terms, Emily Brontë is to me what a marathon runner is to a couch potato. My faith in fact does not stand equal to much. It needs props and a script and costumes to dress up its essential insecurity. Vain indeed may be the thousand creeds that move men's hearts; nevertheless, over the years, I've waffled between three different denominations. Even now, I would only call myself a Christian after all kinds of politically correct throat-clearing. The only thing I *can* say without qualification is that I'm a churchgoer. But even that, ironically, requires a degree of spiritual compromise.

True, my religion is social by nature. The name of its central sacrament, *communion*, says it all. And I live in a very large, potentially alienating city. Belonging to a community of faith reduces and humanizes some of that bigness. At the same time, though, from a purely spiritual standpoint, the social side of churchgoing can be a distraction.

Large urban churches, perhaps in response to accusations of

irrelevance, have become powerhouses of task forces and committees and study groups and outreach initiatives. Of course, there's nothing bad in any of that, and much that is good. But it has become impossible for the wary worshipper to enter the sanctuary without passing at least one bulletin board aflutter with notices urging her to DO SOMETHING. And if she does elect to DO even one thing, it can lead so easily to DOING another and another that church membership becomes a full-time job, and Coffee Hour, as an exhausted friend of mine put it, a series of sixty one-minute meetings.

The tension between faith and works is very like the tension between writing and publishing. Even the act of attending a worship service can necessitate getting over a psychological hurdle. When I first ventured back to church in my late thirties, I practically sneaked into the sanctuary, then hurried away afterwards, speaking to no one.

But just as the point of writing is to be read by others, the point of going to church is to join with others in corporate worship. And yes, both do have the effect of making public what was once intensely private, and of subjecting it to a few external controls. Inspiration meets editor and deadline. Meditation meets the *Book of Common Prayer*.

Nevertheless, we are corporate creatures by nature. We join together and tell each other our secrets. And I *like* going to church. On a good Sunday, I can be deeply moved by the seventeenth-century service that is remarkably similar to the one Emily Brontë would have heard her father conduct. I can be genuinely comforted by the confession and absolution; imaginatively caught up in the symbolic re-enactment of Christ's death and resurrection; spiritually buoyed by the hymns and the benediction.

On a bad Sunday, however, the same service can overwhelm me with arcane ritual, obfuscated theology, all the encrusted crap of organized religion. That's when I know what drove the Haworth parson's daughter out the door of her father's church to seek and find not her father's God but her own.

O God within my breast
Almighty ever-present Deity
Life, that in me hast rest
As I undying Life, have power in Thee

In an earlier age, the words *O God within my breast* would have been choked out from a stake through rising smoke. In the mid-nineteenth century, they took their place in a growing chorus of dissent from the sliced and diced sectarian mess English protestantism had become. Today, their ringing certainty can still admonish this reluctant and distracted churchgoer. If I could say them, just once, with any conviction, I would have no need for church. And as for the oldest fear of all, it would have no power, and no place.

> *There is not room for Death*
> *Nor atom that his might could render void*
> *Since thou art Being and Breath*
> *And what thou art may never be destroyed*

Armed as she was with such a faith, it is no wonder that Emily left behind less than a dozen letters and no daily journal to catalogue her mortal existence. Her mortal existence, in fact, was something she seemed to regard as an inconvenience.

Not that she withdrew sweetly and quietly from the world in the style of her later admirer, Emily Dickinson. Withdraw from the world she most certainly did. But not before in effect slamming a door in its face.

Her rudeness to parsonage visitors was legendary. 'She could or would not look "strangers" in the eyes (meaning nearly everyone without the surname Brontë); stayed hair-raisingly mute in company, or addressed only a cutting or negative handful of words to the persons present.... People harpooned on her brusque replies remembered them with smarting indignation for years afterwards.'[6]

Even her eccentricity of dress seemed aimed to displease. If she had simply wished to be comfortable while walking the moors, she could have adopted a Quakerish plainness. As it was, her look has been described as 'gypsy-like'.[7]

Some Brontë scholars attribute her perversity to a death wish, asserting that she '... saw the impossibility of spiritual wholeness in a shallow world which she despised and utterly shunned.'[8] Others proclaim it a *life*-wish, a longing for the freedom she could have enjoyed in a different time and place, but which was denied her in her own. Seen in this light, her flamboyant dress becomes a way of thumbing her nose at the ladylike fashions adopted by her sisters, and her rudeness a slap in the face to the accommodating demeanour expected of her sex.

I am by no means a Brontë scholar. I've never been to Haworth and I've read *Wuthering Heights* a grand total of twice. As for the huge body of Brontë scholarship that exists, I've barely scratched the surface. But I'm not going to let that keep me from putting forward my own theory about Emily. Because I don't think her contrariness was owing to anything she *wanted*. I think it had to do with what she *was*.

* * *

The act of writing is essentially antisocial. It isn't just a matter of needing to be alone in order to do it, either. The phrase 'a room of one's own' still carries a hint of defiance; and anyone who has ever chosen to write seriously knows there is much more to that room than four walls and a view.

First, there is the practical difficulty of claiming and defending it from the rest of the world. It is no easier today than it was in the Brontës' time to shut a door against loved ones, or to walk out through that door, and keep walking, until a house with all its attendant responsibilities drops from sight. Nor is it a simple thing, in a workaholic society, to leave the office at a reasonable hour each day and risk being labelled 'not a team player'. (It occurs to me that Emily Brontë may have been many things, but a 'team player' was definitely not one of them.) So unless a writer is independently wealthy, she has to strike a rather uneasy bargain with the world in order to support her habit until such time that it can support her.

After a mercifully brief stint as a governess, Emily came back to the parsonage and reinvented herself as a homemaker. She was '…happy to cook and clean and perform the menial functions of the housebound, which offered, by curious paradox, a delinquent's licence to rove up beyond the house and shed female obligations to the four winds … [She] conserved her self in an environment which she could control. Mundane tasks, taking up so little space in her mind, freed her for the life of thought and imagination.' [9]

Years ago, I took a two-month unpaid leave of absence from my day job in order to write my first book. When I returned to work, I agreed with upper management that what I had done did not exactly constitute fast-track behaviour, and took a demotion. I've never considered this a sacrifice. The alternative, sacrificing that room of my own – the time, energy and psychological space that let my writing breathe – would have been tantamount to sacrificing my *self*.

Be yourself. Anyone who was ever a teenager knows how baffling, even paralysing, that injunction can be, whether it comes from a parent, a peer or a magazine aimed at the adolescent market. It doesn't help, of course, that the subtext is usually, *Be the self that is most pleasing and acceptable to us – your parents, your teachers, your peers, your society. Be the self that will never disappoint us, disturb us, frighten or anger us.*

Don't write *Wuthering Heights,* in other words.

Or if you do, prepare to be as alone as it is possible for anyone to be.

And now I can tell that both my feet are on that holy ground which is not only dangerous but familiar. Perhaps dangerous *because* familiar.

It frightens me to think that Emily Brontë died without having the slightest intimation of the praise and renown her novel would one day earn. I'm afraid for myself, of course – projecting my own craving for approval and acceptance onto someone who was so utterly and completely herself as to have no such need.

How do you get there from here? Nobody starts out that self-sufficient, not even Emily Brontë. A young writer will instead write in the way she senses will please her parents, partner and friends. In early days, she might read aloud or submit copies of what she has written to some of these trusted individuals, then gauge from their reaction how well she's doing. Such support systems are an inevitable, probably necessary, part of a writer's development. Emily certainly had one. Her childhood writings were part of an immensely complex story-game she and her siblings kept going into their twenties.

But there comes a point when childish things must be put away.

In 1845, Charlotte Brontë found the notebook in which Emily had been secretly writing her poems. She read them, and in an act that would have required considerable courage, told her sister what she had done. Emily, predictably, was '... furious at this intrusion on her privacy; it took hours to soothe her, days to convince her that such poems merited publication.'[10]

At first glance, Emily's reaction is baffling. Why would she hide writing of the calibre of *No Coward Soul?* Happily, in the end she did consent to publish. So was her initial objection a tease, a case of protesting too much?

No. It was just unfortunate timing on her sister's part. Emily's reluctance to let the world in on her writing was a sign that she no longer needed its approval. She had grown up as an artist. The childhood story-games were over. She would never again collaborate, but would write by and as and for herself alone.

In time, and on her own initiative, she would have shared her work. Charlotte merely caught her before her wings were quite dry.

I'm beginning to think my own are going to stay damp for eternity. It is so *hard* to write strictly by and for oneself. I waste reams of paper, scribbling politely all around what I want to say, skirting, avoiding, minding my manners, employing tact and diplomacy and charm. With everything I write, I have to grow up all over again. Time after time, I have to in effect 'kill' that inner child who desperately wants to please her elders. Time after time, I have to banish from that room of my own all the kind and caring folk who may not be there in the flesh but still manage to make their presence known. The crowd within my breast.

This is not to say that a writer may have no personal loyalties, or must go through life unloving and unloved. Emily Brontë was fiercely loyal to her family. In an act of supreme charity, she nursed her brother through his final illness, very likely thereby contracting the tuberculosis that killed her.

But her first loyalty and the object of her greatest love was the creative act, which was part and parcel of her religious faith.

With wide-embracing love
Thy spirit animates eternal years
Pervades and broods above,
Changes, sustains, dissolves, creates and rears

* * *

Lent is over. Jesus Christ is risen today, so the hymn tells me. I'm not sure what that means, and can't help noticing that it happens every year. In fact, I spend a good part of every year waiting for my God to be born, then waiting for him to die, then waiting for him, in some mysterious way, to be born again.

It's a story I'm told every Sunday, and have been told, one way or another, all my life. I can't even remember hearing it for the first time, though I imagine it got pride of place right up there with Aesop and Disney.

In a way, I've come full circle. Though there have been times when I've struggled to take the story literally and believe it as historical fact, my faith is now, as it once was, a thing of the imagination. Jesus as a fictional character is more alive and real to this fiction writer than any of the crumbling documents that 'prove' he once existed could possibly make him.

But his story is nevertheless a borrowed story, one that can be as 'here and now' or as 'long ago and far away' as I find convenient. It comes equipped with church, and comforting ritual, and the company of other people – all hooks on which to hang my essential solitude. Most of the time, the hooks are worth the compromise.

And so my business with Emily Brontë is concluded. I've come as close to her as I can on this dangerous, sacred ground, and there are still a few crucial paces separating us. There always will be. She's already out the door of the church, on her way to a cold and stony place where I can't follow, there to do what I can't do – find within her own breast her own cold and stony God.

1. *The Brontë Sisters: Selected Poems*, edited by Stevie Davies (1976), 88–89.
2. Daphne du Maurier, *The Infernal World of Branwell Brontë* (1960), 177.
3. Ibid., 173.
4. Ibid., 178.
5. K.D. Miller, *A Litany in Time of Plague* (Erin, Ontario: The Porcupine's Quill, 1994), 117.
6. Stevie Davies, *Emily Brontë: Heretic* (1994), 7–8.
7. Katherine Frank, *A Chainless Soul: A Life of Emily Brontë* (1990), 231.
8. Lyndall Gordon, *Charlotte Brontë: A Passionate Life* (1994), 150.
9. Stevie Davies, *Emily Brontë: Heretic* (1994), 11–12.
10. Phyllis Bentley, *The Brontës* (1969), 86.

Holy Writ

... I seek you eagerly with a heart that thirsts for you and a body wasted with longing for you, like a dry land, parched and devoid of water;[1] ... out of the depths I have called to you;[2] all night long my pillow is wet with tears, I drench my bed with weeping;[3] all my longing lies open before you ... and my sighing is no secret to you ... do not forsake me; ... be not far aloof from me;[4] ... why have you cast me off, why do you hide your face from me?[5] My sight grows dim with looking for your promise and I cry,' When will you comfort me?'[6]

I went through the Psalms, picked out the more anguished lines, pieced them together, then eliminated the words 'Lord' and 'God'. As I had suspected they would, they read like the voiced cry of anyone who has ever suffered unrequited love. There is a feeling of yearning throughout the Psalms, of neediness, almost obsession. At their happiest, they are hymns of praise for the beloved; but that happiness is always short-lived. In just a few verses we're back to: *Where are you? Why won't you talk to me? Why are you so distant when I need you so much?*

The whole heartbreak cycle of the Psalms rings a bell for me as a writer. I have a relationship with writing. I feel about writing much the way I would feel about someone I lived with, someone I loved, someone who could, in large part, make or unmake my happiness. During those times when I can't write, I go through my days outwardly calm but inwardly panicked. I do my job, keep up with the housework, laugh with friends. But none of it is right. How can it be? The relationship that is at the centre of my world has gone wrong.

At first I hesitated to describe writing that way. *The relationship that is at the centre of my world.* Once the words were on paper, I hovered over them, making little jabs at them with my pen. Finally I had to leave them alone, because they were telling the truth.

But it's an odd truth, and an odd relationship. It's the *process* of writing that I love and fight with and need. Not the end product. And certainly not the reader. In fact, unless I put the reader out of my mind completely, I'll never produce anything worth reading.

I encountered that paradox for the first time when I trained as an actor. I was taught to be curiously disbelieving of the audience I could see and hear faintly just a few feet away. I had to cultivate and sustain a belief in the world of the play instead, in the characters that populated that world, and above all in my own character. *The audience will believe in you*, I was taught, *to the exact degree that you believe in yourself.* I've since discovered that it's much the same with writing. I will connect with my reader only when and if I connect with myself. Only when and if I find my voice.

Believe in yourself. Find your voice. There's something smug about those otherwise good bits of advice. They have the glibness of *Take it to the Lord* or *Let go and let God.* Why are both art and religion so crammed with clichés that are meant to elucidate but in fact only baffle? As an actor, a writer and a churchgoer, I've too often found myself in discussion groups where people might as well be babbling away at each other in tongues. So what do I mean when I say I have to *find my voice?*

I'll start with what I don't mean. Years ago I set myself two tasks – writing a novel and at the same time reading everything Daphne du Maurier ever wrote. I wanted to immerse myself in her voice – absorb it through my pores, as I would scented bubble bath. I also wanted, I realize now, to avoid the confrontation with myself that is absolutely necessary to good writing. It was too hard to find my own voice, and too easy to borrow du Maurier's. I was so obsessed with the idea of *being* a writer, in fact, that the necessity of *doing* the work escaped me. (Even though I did produce the novel – a never-to-be-published exhaustion of the adjective that reads kind of like scented bubble bath.)

My voice is *mine*. It isn't borrowed from a favourite author. It doesn't follow fashion. It ignores the market. It knows what it wants to say and says it in the fewest and best words. Its identifying mark is its *authority*. As an actor I was taught that I could do anything on stage – Hamlet's *To be or not to be* soliloquy while naked and standing on my head – provided I did it with *authority*. That is, absolute belief in myself and what I was doing. The difficulty, however, in both acting and writing, is that such authority is not something I can frame and hang on the wall then simply point to as a fixed credential. In everything I write, I have to seek and find my voice as if for the first time. Maybe *discern* is the word I should be using. Because there are so many voices the world would prefer me to use – polite, self-effacing, accommodating, complacent, fashionable, politically correct. It's so easy to get confused and mistake one of them for my own. With everything I write, I must in effect pick my own true voice out of a line-up.

So. Being myself enables me to write and writing enables me to be myself. That kind of thinking used to make me motion-sick in Philosophy 100. And I'm certainly no philosopher. I came to that conclusion back in the days when I would arrive for my Philosophy 100 class fresh from my Acting 100 class. I had just spent an hour learning to play a character with every inch of my being – my memories, my hormones, my elbows and eyelids. But then for the next hour, I was required to crawl up inside my head and view the world through the flat, narrow lens of logic. I have nothing against logic per se. I just don't know what it has to do with tearing up while I watch a sad movie, or being afraid of spiders, or having a screaming orgasm, or laughing till I pee.

Or with writing. Or with why I write. Because what is my *self* exactly? Well, it's a body. A mind. Then there's all my assorted psychological baggage. But it doesn't end there. There's another dimension whose existence I cannot logically prove but in which I believe. In the past ten years or so, I've been exploring that dimension. I feel as if I've discovered a door in my house, hidden behind some wallpaper. The door leads to a room that makes my house suddenly bigger. Roomier.

Writing is my way of expanding my existence to include that room. Of being more fully myself. Writing is the way I pray. As it was for the Psalmist, writing is for me the medium of intimacy with my God.

* * *

When I first started going to church in my late thirties, after decades of no religious exercise, I used to feel a peculiar excitement each week as Sunday drew near. It was kind of like anticipating a lover's visit – looking forward not so much to sex per se as to *intimacy*. That state of being physically, mentally and emotionally *at one* with someone else.

The service of communion is an opportunity for intimacy. As a communicant, I am gradually drawn in to a state of atonement, that is, *at-one*-ment with God, through prayer, confession, absolution, and ng: *Lord, my heart is not proud, nor are my eyes haughty; I do not busy myself with great affairs or things too marvellous for me. But I am calm and quiet like a weaned child clinging to its mother.*[7]

When writing is going wrong, on the other hand, or when I can't write for any length of time, I'm, well, *not myself*. I feel at odds with my own existence. Out of step. Out of joint. Out of place.

Writer's block is just that – a blockage. An obstruction. A barrier between my superficial and my real selves. And though I'm taught that '... neither death, nor life, nor angels, nor principalities, nor powers, nor things present, nor things to come, nor height, nor depth, nor any other creature, shall be able to separate us from the love of God ...'[8] still, when I can't write, I know what the Psalmist meant by the words, 'My God, my God, why have you forsaken me?'[9]

* * *

I have no wish to trivialize the Psalms, certainly not the line imputed to Jesus on the cross. But I do need to take that line down from the cross, so to speak, and, along with the rest of the Bible, make it my own.

Again, I learned this as an actor – how to take a line that nobody heard any more (either because, like 'My kingdom for a horse!' it was too familiar, or, like 'A *handbag?*' it had been definitively delivered by

Dame Edith Evans) and in effect *eat* it. Take it in, absorb it, make it part of my own blood and bones so that when I spoke it, it was alive again and brand new.

A few years ago I took two survey courses in Old and New Testament from the University of Toronto. In both classes, I encountered educated, intelligent individuals who became deeply upset whenever biblical literature was treated as just that – literature. They wanted their Bible to be the literal, irrefutable Word of God. Any attempt to view it critically was taken as an assault both on scripture and on themselves.

I used to wish I could dismiss these folks as unsophisticated and none too bright, but I couldn't. One was a lawyer and one was a stockbroker. And the other was me.

That came as a shock. I did not go into the classroom thinking of myself as a literalist or fundamentalist. And for the most part, I wasn't. I was happy to regard Eden as creation myth and the books of Jonah and Job as allegory. I had no problem deconstructing the Gospels either, in terms of their editorial bias and questionable fact base.

But for all that, I discovered within myself a vestigial lobe of awe for Holy Writ. I couldn't quite bring myself to see the Bible for what it in fact is – a bunch of stuff written by a bunch of people who have been dead for millennia. This was the Good Book, after all. Sacred Scripture. Gospel Truth. Surely it was special. Surely it was a cut above other books. Hell, couldn't it at least glow in the dark?

No. It couldn't. Because I was a writer myself. I knew how the bunny came out of the hat, and I knew it wasn't magic. I had made all the sweaty mistakes writers make, followed all the false leads, ended up in all the dead ends. And though I was willing to admit God into the process, the notion of some ancient scribe going into a trance and producing Automatic Scripture was distasteful and silly.

I still believed in God, and I had no desire to throw the Bible out with the bath water. But if biblical literature came into being the same way my own stories and essays did, where did that leave me? Did that put me on a par with the prophets and the psalmists? And did that make what I wrote Holy Writ?

* * *

I spoke of picking my own voice out of a line-up. The *suspect* voice, in other words. The one I have to differentiate from at least half a dozen others that bear an uncanny resemblance to it. But why *suspect*? What is the crime?

In trying to answer that, I found myself remembering Angela Carter years ago at the Toronto Harbourfront Reading Series announcing that she was going to read what she thought of as her 'very first grown-up story'. What she meant by that, she said, was that it was the first bit of writing she ever did entirely for herself, without giving a damn what anybody else thought of it or of her for having written it.

The story was *The Executioner's Beautiful Daughter*,[10] a tale darker than dark, wickedly funny and merciless in its satire. Each time I read it I feel for its author that envy we all feel for somebody who manages to get away with something. 'Good for you, Angela!' I silently shout. 'Give it to them!'

But what has she gotten away *with*? And who is *them*?

Again, she described *The Executioner's Beautiful Daughter* as the first story she had ever written for herself and no one else. It was a step taken, in other words, one that for her constituted 'growing up'. But it was a particular kind of growing up. It wasn't a debutante's coming-out, approved and applauded by loving authority figures. No, this was an achievement of self, accomplished entirely on her own terms. It was a literary thumbing of her nose at everyone who presumed to have some kind of stake in who she was.

As I said earlier, I have personally known two excellent writers who gave up writing because they were afraid of the pain they might inflict on their loved ones. They were both good, kind people. But while I believed their stated reason for giving up writing, I suspected there was something besides the possibility of hurting others that they were in fact afraid of.

Finding one's voice as a writer is a psychologically subversive act. It marks an end to accommodation, an end to compromise and a defiance in the face of fear. The fear of being alone, that is. Outcast. Outlaw.

I'm not saying that a writer must blow up bridges or neglect her personal hygiene. Nor does she necessarily have to write what is shocking or outrageous or offensive. What she does have to do, however, is tell the truth. Then take the consequences.

The truth shall make you free.[11]

I am not a Christian because I've accepted Jesus as my *personal saviour*. Frankly, I haven't a clue what that means, and the phrase has the utilitarian ring of *personal trainer* or *personal accountant*. I am not a Christian because I think of my baptism as 'proof-of-payment', kind of like a stamp on my hand, that will gain me admittance to Heaven when I die. I am not a Christian because I believe what I recite every Sunday about Jesus sitting on the right hand of God – a phrase that makes me giggle if I think about it too long. I am not a Christian because I believe Jesus is the Son of God. (Am I the Daughter of God? If not, why not?) I am not a Christian because I believe what some people on street corners like to yell at me, namely that Jesus died for my sins. God knows, I can be a real bitch sometimes, but I'm not likely to do anything deserving of crucifixion.

I am a Christian because I am imaginatively hooked on the story of a convicted felon who not only gets away with it, but goes on to be an all-time international best-seller. What is his crime? Growing up. Finding his voice, telling the truth with it and not giving a damn what anybody thinks.

Holy Writ, in other words.

---

1. Psalm 63:1.
2. Psalm 130:1.
3. Psalm 6:6.
4. Psalm 38:9, 21–22.
5. Psalm 88:14.
6. Psalm 119:82.
7. Psalm 131:1–3.
8. Romans 8:38.
9. Psalm 22:1.
10. Contained in Carter, Angela, *Artificial Fire* (1988).
11. John 8:32.

More Than I Thought I Knew

MELINDA BURNS

We went to church and Sunday school every week at the Anglican Church of the Resurrection over on Woodbine Avenue in Toronto. I remember walking there from our house near Coxwell. I liked Sunday School, but then I liked any kind of school. In the summer I went to Vacation Bible school and liked that too. Colouring pictures for Bible stories. Shadrach, Meshach and Abednego come to mind. Daniel in the lion's den. Something about a fiery furnace. And singing 'Jesus wants me for a sunbeam, to shine for him each day. In every way try to please him, at home, at school, at play.' The words come back so easily. 'Jesus loves me, this I know.' I think the songs did comfort me, as did the picture of gentle-eyed Jesus holding a lamb, with his soft hair and robes and his hand held up in blessing. Church was not a bad thing for me. It was a time to get dressed up and walk somewhere as a family, and it took all morning. I found it very dependable.

We moved to the suburbs when I was twelve and I changed from going to Sunday school to going to church, which was much more formal and dreary. The sermons droned on. I was confirmed in the Church of St. Columba and hardly remember a thing about it except that something was 'an outward and visible sign of an inward and spiritual grace'. Why has that phrase stayed with me for forty years? I think I expected more of the whole ceremony after the months of confirmation classes and memorizing so much, and was surprised when nothing really changed. After that I played piano for the Sunday school and maybe taught a class, an obligation I didn't enjoy at all. And as a teenager I went to Young People's, where I remember dancing with a boy in a white shirt and being intoxicated with the smell of his sweat.

The Guelph poet, short story writer and teacher Melinda Burns is one of sixteen authors who responded to my questionnaire concerning the spiritual aspects of the writing life. Hers was one of four responses I chose to reproduce in full.

Religion meant mainly trying to be good, which was my mission in life everywhere – at home, at school, at play. And the older I got, the more of a failure at it I felt. There was no room for anger or bad moods or wanting to jump out of my skin at my parents' questions about my life.

I believed God or Jesus was always watching me and knew everything about me, not unlike my mother. The core of my religious feeling was that I would never be good enough, that essentially I was not good, but if I worked on it all the time – doing what my parents told me without talking back – I might be all right. I might go to heaven when I died.

Since those days of obligatory churchgoing, there has been a significant change in my religious outlook. But it has been fairly evolutionary, a long period of small changes.

I am grateful for the religious instruction I received as a child. It was an important ritual in my life and maybe had more impact on me than I think. If I could have chosen for myself from what I know now, I would have liked more Native American or Buddhist beliefs, especially since my heritage is Native American. The Buddhist view of essential goodness I would also have found very helpful, growing up.

I believe in something larger than myself, something larger than the getting and striving part of me, something that is in all of us and in all of nature, like a Divine Intelligence that knows far more than I do how it all works. I find glimpses of this belief in Taoism and Buddhism and in Native American spirituality as I understand them. In Taoism it has to do with the existence of the 'Way' and with non-interference. Ursula Le Guin wrote in one of her novels, 'There is a Way but you have to find it.' The Quakers say, 'As the way opens, proceed.' In Buddhism, it has to do with 'basic goodness' and Buddha nature, that there is a place in all of us that is wise and knowing and good, that can be trusted. In Native American spirituality it is harmony with nature, a sense of limits, a respect for life in all its forms, a sense that we are a part of the earth and must act in accord with nature. In all three I find a sense of great patience and trust that helps me live my life.

The biggest difference from when I was a child is that I don't think of God as something outside of me. I think of myself as part of God made particular, and of God as being in me, in my deepest self. I wish I had known this when I was growing up. I strove too much to be only good and consequently found myself only bad. I shrank away, put myself away as much as possible. My life seems to be a process of uncovering layers of this self I put away, like Michelangelo freeing his figures from stone. I think that's why his sculptures, *The Prisoners,* moved me so much when I saw them in Florence last year.

I would say spirituality is part of my life now but formal religion is not. I like the idea of church – the gathering of people, the singing together, the focus on matters of the spirit, but I really can't abide the dogma. I sometimes go to a meditation group that meets on Sunday mornings at the yoga centre a few blocks from my house. We sit in silence for thirty minutes and then there is a talk and a discussion. I like that much better than church, especially the sitting in silence. With a little singing thrown in, that's the kind of 'service' I could be happy with.

I learned Transcendental Meditation in (where else?) California in about 1975 and I've been meditating off and on ever since. TM involves a secret mantra, which I still remember but don't use. My meditation now is more Buddhist, based on following the breath. I've been meditating regularly every morning for about five years. It was more sporadic before that. When my husband and I started having trouble that led to separation, I made a place for myself in our house when he moved out – a writing/meditation room where I could sit quietly and gather strength, or find peace in the midst of not knowing what to do or what would happen. I made an altar of pictures and objects that have significance to me, and I would light sage or sweetgrass as my native ancestors might have long ago, thank my ancestors for bringing me to life and for the day, and ask for help. Then I would meditate.

I meditate now sitting on my bed facing the window where the sun comes through in the morning. I read something inspiring – I just finished *Stumbling Towards Enlightenment* by Geri Larkin who is a Zen teacher. Then I sit for fifteen minutes and try to stay with my breath or the sounds that float in from outside, coming back over and over when my thoughts take me away. I also do a form of meditation before I go to sleep which is to think of five things I'm grateful for in the day that's ending.

I could describe most activities in my life in spiritual terms given half a chance – reading, talking to friends, my work as a therapist, going to help my mother, feeding the cats, making soup. I think the spiritual *is* what we do and how we do it. It is everything. Writing, certainly. I don't think it's a coincidence that my writing room and meditation room were the same. Writing is like meditation for me, a way of being aware, more present, of finding the Way, probing the mystery. Not to understand it so much as to participate in it, appreciate it, consider why we're here, how to live, how to love.

I write every day for at least half an hour. This is my 'writing practice' which is as much spiritual as literary for me. Sometimes I work on something specific, like a story. Sometimes it's just whatever wants to be written. I've had various rituals for writing. For years, I did three pages in the morning on whatever came to me. For one month in the summer, I wrote a poem a day. A few years ago I scheduled writing time with the Writing Goddess, a muse I invented who didn't care what I wrote as long as I showed up.

I think committing to a daily half-hour minimum does render the act of writing 'sacred'. (I once read a definition of 'sacred' as 'generating strength'.) It says to me that it's inviolable, not subject to the vicissitudes of the day. Which is a bit scary – what if I can't? So far I can and do. I like taking the risk, like marriage. It says, 'I take this seriously. I won't make excuses.'

Because I write regularly, I don't think a lot about inspiration as such. I would describe it as a gift, a breakthrough of something unplanned, unthought, an opening where I see something I haven't seen before or things come together as I hadn't expected. It comes from showing up and doing the work, and letting go, both. It comes from that place in me that knows so much more than I realize, that needs a vehicle, like a poem or a story, or writing through a problem. I'm not in control of it but I can put myself in the way of it, and hope.

I think all writers travel in worlds beyond the one we're usually aware of. I start in the world of the senses, and it seems the more I'm grounded in this world, in the details, the more likely I am to enter the other world of knowing something more than I thought I knew, or alternatively, of not knowing something I thought I knew. Finding the opening.

I have written nearly every day since someone gave me a journal when I was twelve. Even the day I gave birth to my daughter I sat up in bed that evening to get down on paper as much of the experience as I could before I lost it. I don't know what this compulsion is. It didn't come from any driving ambition to be a writer when I was growing up, and I didn't identify myself as a writer for decades, even though I filled notebook after notebook with my thoughts and feelings. I would classify this as a need to reflect, to step back or out for a time and look at what I'm doing, where I'm going. And a need to make something of it — a poem, a story, something that brings it all into clearer focus.

In a spiritual sense I believe I'm here, we're all here, to be the best we can of who we are, to use whatever gifts we have, to tell our particular version of what we see and experience, and to experience it more deeply and clearly. Writing helps me with all that. For some people it might be making music or painting, or raising children, or organizing communities. For me, it's writing. That's my vehicle and my instrument, my tool, my work, my play.

If I couldn't write I would feel less alive. I wouldn't be dead but something would be deadened. I could still read to feed my soul, but writing is like exercise to my soul, like dance, movement, muscle toning. I would be flabby of soul, underused, neglected, without writing. I'm a much better person to be around when I'm writing — funnier, more generous, happier, more interested in what's around me, more spontaneous.

I believe society needs me to go on writing, just as it needs all of us to do the work we're here for. But particularly society needs artists and writers, people who listen to themselves past the immediate wants and thoughts to the deeper place of the soul, who love words and seek to bring out their meanings rather than empty them into clichés and catch-phrases and advertising slogans. I think society needs people to write about what it means to be human — the miracles and redemption that come through human acts and interactions. It comforts me to know there are people who do this and I can't think that we can have too many of them. I would classify the need as one of wholeness, of bringing to light that which must never be lost, our humanness, with all its light and dark. A need for true mirrors so we don't forget the immense possibilities of life, for good and evil.

I believe the consequences of that need not being met are a flat sameness overlaying us, a lethargy, a hopelessness and despair in the soul, that would do us in as surely as any ecological or political disaster. I believe writers keep spirit and soul alive.

Whit's End[1]

I wish I'd had a more interesting childhood. If I'd been just a little less well-behaved, or my family just a little more dysfunctional, if there had been even one dark, shameful secret in our ancestral past or a demented cousin or two kept locked in a coal cellar, I might not have to work so hard as a fiction writer. But my father had a steady job, my mother never missed a Home and School meeting, my brother was a Queen's Scout and I once won a good citizenship prize from the Imperial Order of the Daughters of the Empire.

What's more, when I walked along the sidewalk in the summer catching drips with my tongue from an orange Popsicle, no Miss Havisham spied on me from behind dingy lace curtains. At night when I did my homework in my room, no first Mrs Rochester raved in the attic above my head. We didn't even have an attic, come to think of it. The first Mrs Rochester would have had to do her raving in the rec room, whose fake wood panelling and snooker table would have robbed her of much of her Gothic effect.

And I craved Gothic in those days. My reading of choice ran along the lines of Poe's *The Premature Burial*. My favourite TV programs were Rod Serling's *Twilight Zone* and Boris Karloff's *Thriller*. At the age of eleven, when I saw the film of Harper Lee's *To Kill a Mockingbird*, this first whiff of Southern Gothic produced a yearning in me that was almost physically painful. I wanted to be Scout. I wanted Scout's life, her neighbourhood, her family, her accent. I wanted her friend Dill. (Recently, when I discovered that Dill is in fact a portrait of the young Truman Capote, who was Harper Lee's childhood friend, I wanted him and everything that went with him all over again.)

But it's time for a reality check. I have never in fact been to the Deep South. Chances are, if I ever did go down there, the humidity and mosquitoes would send me packing for home in minutes. And do I really want to be a motherless nine-year-old? A tomboy forced into dresses and forever teetering between innocence and its loss?

I think what I actually want is the mystery that infuses Scout's existence. She spends the last summers of her childhood trying to lure Arthur 'Boo' Radley, the neighbourhood recluse, out of the house he hasn't left in decades. Generations of children have mythologized and demonized Boo, to the point that when he finally does emerge, a kind of innocence is lost. Scout looks at the source of all the stories and sees nothing but simple, frightened Arthur. '… as I gazed at him in wonder the tension slowly drained from his face. His lips parted into a timid smile, and our neighbour's image blurred with my sudden tears.'[2]

When I say I want to be Scout and live Scout's life in Scout's world, I'm talking about everything up to but not including that moment. Because something in me wants not Arthur but *Boo* Radley. The presence felt, but unseen. The mystery intact.

* * *

I once started to write a story called 'Escape from the Planet of the Church People'. That's as far as I got – just the title.

It was during the year after I was confirmed, which would have made me thirty-nine or forty. (I was a spiritual late bloomer.) All that year, I was in an ecstasy of churchiness, attending mass twice a week, signing up for activities and generally acting the part of the seed that sprouts quickly but withers in the sun because it hasn't had time to put down roots.[3]

The 'sun' that just about did me in was a parish conference planning committee that I was asked to join. Somehow, despite my showing up at the place with such embarrassing frequency, it had escaped my notice that a church is, among other things, a building full of people. So when the committee members started acting like people, airing ancient grudges, cherished resentments and personal agendas at these meetings that I had thought would constitute a spiritual group hug, I went into shock. I think I actually expected Jesus to storm in and start overturning tables the way he's supposed to do at times like this.

Well, it didn't happen. Instead, we got through the committee meetings somehow, planned and held the parish conference somehow, then went on coming to church with each other. Somehow.

A decade has gone by, and I haven't gotten any farther with writing 'Escape from the Planet of the Church People'. I'm not sure I ever will. I've made good friends at my church, and I've learned to avoid committee work. Besides, I'm as lazy spiritually as I am physically. I won't exercise unless I join a class with an instructor beating time, and I'll neglect my spiritual self unless I take it to church once a week.

Which means, I guess, that I'm a practising Christian. The phrase makes me smile. 'Christian' is true insofar as I am endlessly fascinated by the Jesus story. But I don't take it as Gospel truth, so to speak. My Creed begins and ends with *I believe in God.* After that, it's anybody's guess. And 'practising' sounds as if I'm going over and over the same few notes or dance steps, trying to get them right.

Well, every Sunday morning I do listen to the same story being told in the same words, meanwhile chiming in with the same responses. I stand, sit or kneel on the same cues every week, then eat a tiny, symbolic meal identical to the one served up the Sunday before. Though I'm not sure if I'm 'getting it right', or even what that means in this context, the repetition itself is reassuring. The familiar routine of the liturgy lends some perspective to my spiritual highs and lows. Even now, I can still enjoy bursts of religious puppy love, when every word or note of the service is a little treat just for me. But then there are stretches of spiritual boredom when God is a remote abstraction and going to church a chore. It's not unlike what happens in a long-term sexual relationship. There's a cycle of passion involved, and low periods when all you do is go through the motions, trusting the good times to roll again soon.

In spiritual terms, the 'good times' for me are intensely personal and private. The social and active sides of church membership appeal to me less and less as time passes. I don't mean to criticize people who find their spiritual fulfilment in human relationships, or who attempt to address society's ills through church work. I'm just saying that if I could express my religious self in a single gesture, it would be neither to shake hands nor to roll up my sleeves, but to kneel.

* * *

When I say I'm endlessly fascinated by the Jesus story, I'm not referring to the more spectacular parts of it. The accounts of him walking on water[4] and stretching a loaf of bread to feed thousands[5] are fables, as far as I'm concerned. They have great symbolic value; but to take them literally is to render Christ a magician or party trickster.

More and more, it's the small, very human and thoroughly believable details that hook my imagination and won't let it go: Jesus arguing with his mother about wine at a wedding;[6] Jesus grilling fish over a fire on the beach;[7] Jesus crouching to write with his finger in the dust.[8] Ironically, if anything is ever going to convince me of the divinity of Christ (and this is a major stumbling block for me – one that makes me technically non-Christian) it will be neither the miracles nor the resurrection but one of these utterly human little bits of business. They serve to bring Jesus into such sudden, sharp focus that I almost wish the New Testament ended with those piquing final words in the Gospel of John: *There is much else that Jesus did. If it were all to be recorded in detail, I suppose the world could not hold the books that would be written.*[9] If that isn't an exit line, I don't know what is. Trouble is, the show doesn't end there. Instead, the supporting cast stay on stage to perform what I think of as literature's greatest anti-climax – the Book of Acts.

Acts tells the story of the early Christian movement struggling to take hold. It is, among other things, a story about petty politics and personal agendas. People, in other words. A friend once described the events in Acts as being 'kind of like church'. With a sinking feeling, I had to agree.

* * *

The last church committee I ever served on was a Worship Committee. A Buddhist friend of mine expressed some puzzlement about this. 'A worship *committee?*' he said. 'But isn't worship what the place is supposed to be all *about?*' He had a point, but it took me a while to see it.

Frankly, the Worship Committee had a certain cachet. I was flattered to be asked to join a small group of parishioners clustered round the Rector. And maybe this time, I told myself, things would be different.

They were. People were friendly. They respected each other's points of view and made a sincere effort to be mature and professional. Minutes of meetings were circulated promptly. Lovely refreshments were served.

It was all so very nice, in fact, that it took me a while to notice that the main topic of discussion, the one we inevitably returned to whether it was on the agenda or not, was furniture. The arranging of furniture.

Of course, we didn't call it that. We were talking about the *altar,* after all. Specifically, whether the altar should remain in the sanctuary, requiring communicants to walk toward it, then veer off to left or right to return to their pews, or whether it should be situated in the nave, closer to the centre of the church, where those receiving communion could stand around it in a circle. Both arrangements had been tried out in the past few years, the latter involving a second altar, on wheels, that could be rolled into place for a circle service, then pushed back into a corner for a more traditional Eucharist. No one was happy. The circle people wanted to be allowed to form their circles more than a few times a year. They felt, they said, marginalized. The traditional approach-then-veer-off people, on the other hand, regarded an altar on wheels as undignified. They felt their church was being desecrated, and they themselves assaulted.

During this same time period, this same congregation managed to sponsor and support two Muslim refugee families from Somalia, cutting through thickets of red tape and all but dodging bullets in the process. We also conducted a controversial discussion of homosexuality, eventually sending a letter to the justice minister stating our support for the inclusion of the words 'sexual orientation' in the Charter of Rights and Freedoms. In both cases, there were those who cheered and those who wept. But in both cases, we managed to remain a community.

When it came to where to put the altar, however, the congregation was bitterly and irreconcilably divided. The Circlists believed that only by eyeballing each other across a centrally placed Eucharist could they achieve true communion. The Veerists maintained that they approached the Lord's Table in order to commune with the *Lord*, thank you very much, and had time enough during Coffee Hour to love their neighbour.

The one point that even the most adamant Circlist had to concede was that the congregation was too large to form a single circle. Instead, during nave altar services, a series of circles had to form, then disperse, then form again, creating confusion and traffic jams. People complained of not knowing exactly where to stand (despite duct-tape markers on the floor); of being overlooked by confused servers, with the result that they received the Body of Christ but not the Blood, or perhaps Blood sans Body; of having to fight through crowds of incoming faithful on their way back to their pews.

The Worship Committee took all these concerns to heart. We tried opening up a little side chapel during circle services, so those who preferred to approach-and-veer could do so. But congestion remained a problem, with departing Circlists colliding with approaching Veerists, and cries of *Foul!* all round.

The Rector confessed himself heartsick over the division of his flock. Desperate for compromise, the Worship Committee cast about for ways to make the circles a little less hazardous. Should a bell be rung when a circle had been completely served with bread and wine, thus signalling it to disperse? Who would ring the bell? How would they know when to ring it? Could someone signal the bell-ringer? But who would signal the signaller? And in order to keep Circlist/Veerist confrontation to a minimum, could some parishioners be designated as traffic police? Was this perhaps a way to get the Youth Group more involved?

My mind began to wander during these meetings. I found myself reflecting on the sheep dog trials I had watched at the Royal Winter Fair, wherein Border collies had successfully herded gaggles of geese over little bridges, through little tunnels and up and down little sets of stairs. Then I remembered the part in *Gulliver's Travels* about the two kingdoms slaughtering each other for centuries because they couldn't agree on the correct way to eat a boiled egg.

I began to understand my greater affinity for a transcendent, as opposed to an immanent, God. And I retired from church committee work forever.

I realize that what all this says about me isn't entirely flattering. I'm taught that the kingdom of heaven is *at hand.* Literally. To my right and to my left in the pew, in the person of my neighbour. I'm taught that I should look at my neighbour and try to see God. But I just don't seem to be hard-wired that way. And I confess that I don't really *want* God to be my neighbour. I want God to be Boo Radley.

* * *

Maybe what all this is adding up to (besides the fact that I'm something of a curmudgeon) is that I'm a writer. A writer is by nature somebody who doesn't quite fit in. And if I'm honest with myself, I'll admit that I don't really *want* to fit in.

As a child and adolescent, I would have sold my soul to be an unobtrusive member of the gang. The rituals of ordinariness were like complicated dance steps for me. I could sometimes catch the rhythm and fake it for a while, but sooner or later, I'd stumble and reveal myself as the misfit I was. Now, I treasure whatever it is that keeps me at a slight remove. In a way, my survival depends on it. I know most people lead perfectly satisfactory lives without ever feeling the need to write a story or novel or poem. But it's like knowing that a fish can breathe in water. I *know*, but do not *understand* how such a thing is done. And if I tried it myself, I'd drown.

But this is getting a bit precious. Writers, after all, are people. We hold down jobs, raise kids, go to the movies and sometimes even go to church. Still, we have a peculiar relationship with the ordinary stuff of our lives.

Once or twice a year, I wake up in a strange bed. For several seconds I look around me at bedroom furniture I've never seen before. Through the open door I can see a hallway, but I have no idea where it leads. Then, very gradually, recognition seeps back in. This is *my* bed. My bedroom. The hall leads to the rest of the apartment. My apartment.

The strangeness was not in the surroundings but in my half-awake perception of them. And for a few seconds I managed, to a terrifying degree, to do the thing that as a writer I must do with the stuff of my experience. I must take the familiar and make it strange. But it's not as simple as waking up in a strange bed. I have to *make* the bed strange.

Perhaps it would be better to say that I have to *return* it to its original strangeness. Or better still to speak not of strangeness but of newness. The writer must somehow take what is old and make it new. Whatever I'm writing about must, in my hands, be *born again*.

That phrase can make me cringe. I'm particularly irritated by those relentlessly cheerful souls who manage to smell me out in any crowd and pummel me with the news that they're *born again*. It isn't the concept that I object to. The concept resonates deeply with my writing life. And as for the rest of my life, I happen to believe that I must, as Jesus tells Nicodemus he must,[10] be born again. But it's not a matter of one quick epiphany and bang! you're born again. To re-evaluate and if necessary change one's entire existence in light of some new truth is neither quick nor easy. It can be downright terrifying. Which is what bothers me about the glassy-eyed good cheer of some born-again Christians. Do they *like* being stripped of their complacency, of everything they take for granted? Do they *like* having their hoarded possessions, pampered

appearances and meticulously cultivated social and professional net-
works assessed as so much trash? I don't. And when I say I *believe* I must
be born again, it's kind of like believing in Boo Radley. I'm much more
comfortable when he stays inside his house so I can spin stories about
him. I don't really want to be there when he emerges, and turns out to be
my neighbour. The lonely one I've no time for. Or my colleague at work.
The one I gossip about. Or the beggar on my street. The one I pretend
not to see.

When it comes to writing, if my subject matter is to be 'born again',
that is, freshened and made new, it must undergo a process every bit as
unsettling and fraught with failure. First, I must *look* at it. Really *look* at
it, with cold and alien eyes. The way I look at my bedroom furniture
during those terrifying, half-awake seconds. I have to try for absolute
objectivity (impossible, I know, but I still have to try) – objectivity
stripped of sentimentality, common decency, societal norms, good
manners or anything else we file under N for Nice or P for Politically
Correct.

I have to remake the world, cell by cell and particle by particle. Otherwise, I risk producing the kind of fiction that cushions the reader with
cliché, in effect saying, 'Oh well, you know how *men* are,' or bolsters
them with assumption: 'Of course, we *know* that no mother would do
such a thing to her child.' That's not writing. It's upholstery.

*　*　*

I am, despite the whine with which I began this essay, grateful for the
relatively healthy and stable atmosphere in which I grew up. And I don't
for a moment think I would be a better or more prolific writer if my
childhood and adolescence had been the stuff of sexual gothic. No matter how humdrum or bizarre a writer's past, using it as raw material for
autobiographical fiction is always difficult. Dangerous, in fact. And the
danger lies not so much in riling one's relatives as in mistaking good
therapy for good writing.

I derived tremendous therapeutic value from writing the stories in
my second book, *Give Me Your Answer*. Before I could take a single step
in the direction of fictionalizing my past, I had first to reexamine its
facts. This was particularly true of the stories that dealt with my parents.

It has always interested me that, of the Ten Commandments, only two are expressed in positive terms. One of these is to keep the Sabbath holy. The other is to honour one's father and one's mother. I discovered, in writing *Answer*, that to 'honour' someone means neither to worship nor to sentimentalize them. It means, essentially, to *look* at them. To *see* them. I had first to acknowledge the degree to which I had deified or demonized these two primal beings, my father and my mother. Then I had to try to see through all that to the human reality. When I did, I discovered that chains of anger and resentment that had bound me for years were in fact so much cobweb.

Well, wonderful as that was, it had nothing to do with good writing. An insightful priest or psychiatrist could have helped me get to the same place in my personal development without my having written a word. So if my mental health was enhanced by my second book, it was a pure bonus. For me. Not for the book. And not for its reader.

Which is why I am dismayed when fiction is praised for anything other than the quality of its writing – when it is lauded for doing some kind of job, like *exposing the plight of* or *giving voice to* or *raising awareness of*. A book is not a can opener. Its value does not lie in its ability to do anything except invite me to fall in love with its language.

* * *

I think I go to church because I want to fall in love with God. And while a beautifully conducted service can just about get me there, church itself and church life can sometimes act like a bucket of cold water.

Communion vs. community. Some would say I've completely missed the point. And maybe they would be right. At the very least, I don't think I was entirely fair in my dismissal of The Book of Acts. Acts is essentially about the Holy Spirit, that late-arriving member of the Trinity that manages to prick my conscience every time it's mentioned. The Holy Spirit represents the very thing I'm not very good at. Other people, that is. Putting up with them. Forgiving them. Loving them. It's all so hard. And so necessary.

The arrival of the Holy Spirit is celebrated in my church a few weeks after Easter, and initiates the season of Pentecost. The first Sunday of Pentecost used to be called Whitsunday, and I wish it still was. 'Whit' means wit – not in the Wildean sense, but in the sense of imagination. Perception.

Seeing what's in front of me, in other words. Boo in Arthur, and Arthur in Boo. Their essential strangeness. Their inherent mystery.

---

1. Some sections are taken from my article *Whit's End,* published in the *Integrator,* 99:4.
2. Harper Lee, *To Kill a Mockingbird* (1960), 273.
3. Matthew 13:5.
4. Mark 6:48.
5. Mark 6:41–44.
6. John 2:4.
7. John 21:9–14.
8. John 8:6.
9. John 21:25.
10. John 3:1–8.

Toward Jerusalem

I'm writing this because I can't write. I've done everything else I can do. The apartment is spotless, my shoes are all polished, my tax receipts are in order months before they need to be, I'm so caught up with my correspondence that half the world owes me a letter, and, *mirabile dictu,* I've actually read the latest issues of the literary magazines I subscribe to.

But now all my diverting tasks are done. I roam the apartment like my own ghost. Stare out windows at the same view I've had for twenty years. Study furniture I've had even longer with a fixity that verges on Zen. Peer into the fridge every ten minutes as if expecting the contents to have transformed themselves into something more appetizing.

Except I have no appetite. I'm as peevish as an invalid, petty and self-absorbed. The small ordinary things of my life are suddenly monstrous. I dwell on tiny slights, analyse and re-analyse the most innocent exchanges with friends and colleagues.

And all the time, I'm equal parts tortured and tantalized by a story that is nudging the surface of my consciousness. I know it's there. I can feel its movement like a ripple, can sometimes catch a glimpse of its shadowy shape. But I can't make it rise.

Not for lack of trying. Writer's block is not paralysis. It can actually be marked by a flurry of activity that looks very much like writing – witness this essay. But essay-writing, though no easier than the writing of fiction, is more accessible to me during these dry spells. In an essay, I write *about* something. I examine facts. Make notes. Walk all around my subject, trying to see it from every possible angle. It's a deliberate effort, very much under my conscious control. Yes, the imagination is employed, but more or less as *sous-chef* to the intellect.

When it comes to fiction, the reverse is true. A story begins with a remembered facial expression or gesture or snatch of overheard conversation – something I simply can't get out of my mind. In time (I should say, in its *own* time) the memory becomes a character, or a small group of characters, whom it is my job to try to get to know. It's not unlike moving into a community, or walking into a room full of people, and trying to become one of them. It's tricky. They're neither puppets nor slaves. If I try to force or manipulate them, if I try to make them act against their true natures, they will resist and finally elude me. In order to come to know them, I have to respect their autonomy, and their privacy. Which is why I'm frequently the last to know what my stories are about.

If this is sounding a bit strange, it is. And I don't mean to deny the hard, conscious, technical work that does go into the writing of fiction. But a story in progress has a life of its own. And it tends to grow up and away from its author. Once I've published a story, it can be as alien and remote-seeming to me as a remembered dream. Yes, I know it's *my* dream, that it came from me. But it feels more like something that *happened* to me.

When I'm blocked, I begin to question whether such a thing will ever happen to me again. And the writing I do manage to do is driven less by love and more by fear: *Have I dried up? Was my little bit of success a fluke? What am I going to do for the rest of my life?*

∗ ∗ ∗

On my tax form, my writing income is classed as 'other'. It is large enough to come to the attention of Revenue Canada, but still small enough to earn me the unfortunate title of 'hobbyist'. I write most often in the early morning, for an hour or two before I have to start getting ready for work. Like many artists, I need to support myself with a day job that is unrelated to my art.

Put plainly, the facts of the matter do seem to make me out as someone for whom writing is a pleasant diversion, kind of like golf or bird-watching, with the added advantage of earning me a few extra dollars. But the withdrawal symptoms I described earlier would probably not accompany a sudden inability to spy on birds. Nor is it the extra income (low and extremely sporadic) that I miss when I'm blocked. I do many things when I write, but rendering unto Caesar is not one of them. In fact, in recent years I've come to realize that writing is my way of rendering unto God. It's the way I pray.

That said, I must admit that if I could avoid the words *pray* and *prayer,* I would. They actually make my skin crawl. They're associated in my mind with the sentimentality of 'Christopher Robin Is Saying His

Prayers', and those kitschy paintings of little tots kneeling beside their beds, back flaps of their sleepers adorably unbuttoned.

Even as a child, I hated the babyishness of 'Now I lay me down to sleep....' These days, as a middle-aged *nouveau*-churchgoer, I still have to push myself with prayer. Every Sunday, I do kneel with the rest of the congregation and dutifully respond, 'Lord, hear our prayer' when God is petitioned on behalf of the youth group, the environment and war-torn Wherever. But it's still vaguely embarrassing, and essentially unreal.

So why do I bother? For years, I struggled to be an atheist, only giving it up when I realized I was denying my true nature. But believing in God complicates my life, as any relationship does. I can't just sign a statement of faith and walk away. I have to deal on a regular basis with this entity I have acknowledged.

I'm not sure when I finally made the connection. I never consciously decided to pray by writing, or to write in order to pray. In fact, years ago when I used to set aside a time for prayer first thing every morning, I would sit at my desk struggling *not* to pick up my pen, *not* to think about my latest story. After a while, I would start to wonder what I was doing wrong. Why I couldn't feel that wonderful sense of completeness I had heard and read about. That feeling of being fully present in the moment. As it was, I felt fragmented. Distracted.

Finally, when my mind refused to stop wandering, I would give up and just let myself write. That's when I would come into my own. My muscles would relax, my imagination would open, and I would begin an exercise of pure, concentrated joy.

* * *

All right. That explains prayer. But what's this church thing? Why, on a Sunday morning, do I not just stay home and write? Good question. One I'll probably struggle to answer every Sunday morning for the rest of my life.

One reason, quite simply, is that I'm a Christian, and Christian worship of whatever stripe is interactive. I didn't, for instance, baptize myself. Someone had to dip his fingers in water, then touch them to my hair. Similarly, when I was confirmed, I felt the weight of a bishop's hand on my head. Every week now at a certain point in the service, I fumble my prayer book out of the way and clasp the hands of my pew mates, wishing them the peace of Christ. A few minutes later I kneel, raise my hands to allow a disc of bread to be pressed into my palm, then wait for a cup of wine to be put to my lips.

Looked at objectively, it's every bit as touching and absurd as I suppose the practices of any religion can appear. And whenever I worship, I can be alternately moved and embarrassed by what I'm doing.

Furthermore, I don't consider my faith to be the one path, or even the preferred path, to God. When I say, 'I'm a Christian', I'm making a statement that is as much sociological as anything else. Chances are, if I had been born in Japan, I might describe myself as Buddhist, and follow that very different path in order to reach exactly the same destination.

So the question remains: If writing is the way I pray, and if Christian worship is no better or worse than any other kind, why do I go to church?

Partly, I must admit, out of habit. It's been nine years now, and I've put down roots in the church that is a fifteen-minute walk from my apartment building. Not that I just wandered into it one day because it was handy. In my late thirties, when I found I could no longer deny my basically Christian bent, I followed my baby-boomer consumer instincts and went shopping for a house of worship.

The Presbyterian service I remembered from my childhood was calm and dignified, but to my eyes lacked beauty. Also, its point of departure seemed to be avoidance of anything remotely Catholic. Needless to say, this made the colour and drama of Roman Catholicism very appealing to me as an adolescent. As an adult, however, I simply could not reconcile that church's sexual politics with my own. Then there was the whole happy-clappy Pentecostal side of the family, the very thought of whose speaking in tongues, fainting in the Spirit and hand-pumping fellowship made me want to run and hide.

In the Anglican church (or the Episcopalian, or the Church of England, depending on your address) I found an intriguing jumble of tradition and innovation. On any given Sunday, I might hear a female priest lead us in the words '... Who for us men ... came down from heaven....' And although the newer prayer book contains the phrase 'interstellar space,' the service still includes the solemn closing of little gates to keep the street dogs of seventeenth-century London from swarming the altar and devouring the Body of Christ.

(In the film *Hannah and Her Sisters,* a character voices his belief that if Jesus came back today, he'd never stop throwing up. Well, I happen to think he'd never stop laughing.)

What can I say? I like going to church. I've made friends there. I enjoy the music. It's become part of my week, part of my life.

Except I could have gotten all that by joining a glee club or taking up tai chi. So once again, what does church offer me that I can't get somewhere else?

In trying to answer that question, I began to wonder seriously if I *could* answer it. Or if the answer might turn out to be 'nothing'. Then I remembered that I am a writer of stories. And whenever I go to church, I am told a story, one that contains seven of the most intriguing words ever written: ... *he set his face resolutely toward Jerusalem.*[2]

Though the specific quote is from the gospel of Luke, the moment described is one that occurs in all four of the accounts of the life of Christ. Jesus has been teaching and healing in the small towns around Jerusalem. News of his growing popularity and revolutionary message have reached the religious establishment in the capital, who have essentially put a price on his head. He has a choice. He can stay on the fringes, maybe soften his rhetoric a little, keep his head down and his nose clean and likely die of old age. Or, he can confront his accusers on their own turf, tell his truth to their faces and in effect commit suicide.

There is something in this that speaks to me as a writer, especially when I'm blocked. I need to examine and reexamine the story whose crisis point is that moment. Yes, I could stay home Sunday mornings and read the story for myself. But it's better if I take it in bit by bit, throughout the year. Hear it told and read and sung and talked about by different people who see it differently. Because every time I think I've gotten to the bottom of it, the bottom rings hollow. It's a story that grows as I grow, ages as I age. The more I get to know it, the more complicated and mysterious and at times terrifyingly simple it becomes.

* * *

Beside my desk is a filing cabinet whose bottom drawer is full of good starts – embryonic stories, a novel, a children's book – projects I began years or even decades ago. When things are going well, I think of this as my spare parts drawer, where I can find characters, incidents, tiny details of time or place to work into whatever I'm writing. But when I'm blocked, that drawer seems more like a box of broken toys or stopped watches. Much as I would like to fix them and get them going again, I can't.

Every one of them represents a kind of death, though not necessarily an ending. They're all stuck for a time in what I think of as the Easter Saturday of the creative process. The time between death and resurrection. Despair and hope. Failure and triumph. In other words, the time of the tomb.

That's where I am right now. I've just published my second collection of short stories. Right now, I'm wrapping up this book of essays. And soon, for the first time in over seven years, I'll have no major writing project on my plate. I've been through my bottom drawer of good starts twice, three times, looking for inspiration. Nothing comes to life. I've toyed with the idea of writing a murder mystery. Started one once, years ago. Tried to pick it up where I left off. Can't.

There's nothing for it. I'm in the tomb, for as long as Easter Saturday is going to last. Days. Weeks. Years. Maybe forever. Yes, that has been known to happen.

But as I said before, something is nudging my consciousness. Though I call it a 'story', it could be anything – a novel, a play. Or maybe even something other than writing. A stint of teaching, perhaps. Or travel. Or study. I just don't know. And the not knowing produces in me a maddening combination of restlessness and inertia.

It's small comfort to remind myself that I got here on my own initiative. That I took a risk in persevering with that second book, many of whose stories are based on memories of my childhood. From the first, *Give Me Your Answer* was plagued with false starts and failure. At one point, I decided to abandon it altogether. The choice, as I saw it, was to write dishonestly and innocuously, or to tell the truth, thereby possibly inflicting pain. I didn't want to do either. So I chose to do nothing.

When I informed my editor, John Metcalf, of my non-decision, he responded in a letter I will some day frame. As it is, I pull it out of its file a few times a year and reread it.

Family. The old battle-ground. You say in your letter.... 'I was shying from the danger and pulling punches for the simple reason that certain people are still alive and I don't live in a vacuum.'

I'm suggesting to you ... that [family] is what you ought to be writing about. And that you're 'shying from' that subject matter from honourable and decent motives. But you are a writer. That's what you do. That's what you are. We've all had to face this struggle if we're writing autobiographically.... But to not do it is a cop out. To not do it is to assume essentially bourgeois values. What's really important is for your work to sparkle and to last. You won't connect with other people unless you connect with the primal material of your life and wrestle it to the ground with elegant and powerful language.

In life I much respect politeness, self-effacement, good manners, a surface affability. All necessary stuff. But in art?

That's a different world with different values and different demands. And the unpalatable truth is that if you wish to be important as a writer your allegiance must not be to people but to the perfected arrangement of words on paper.[3]

A tall order. Which I took. I wrote the book, and I wrote it honestly. Now it remains to be seen whether it will live on in such a way as to justify the pain of its becoming.

This is, for me, what gives those words *he turned his face resolutely toward Jerusalem* their chill factor. It's not so much the crucifixion that Jesus is risking. And it's not even the resurrection either, though the hugeness and strangeness of that is frightening enough. When he turns toward Jerusalem, he is risking the tomb. The in-between time when he can't go forward and he can't go back. When all he can do is wait for something, or perhaps nothing, to happen.

* * *

I suspect many people will take exception to the way I look at the Jesus story. The way I make it so very much my own. Well, frankly, I can't do anything else. I must either take it personally or leave it alone.

Years ago, when I was trying to be an atheist, what held me back was an emotional attachment to Jesus. I was quite ashamed of this at the time. I considered it childish and weak, much like sucking my thumb or sleeping with a teddy bear.

But I couldn't kick the habit. I could neither deny my feelings for fairest Lord Jesus, nor dismiss him from my world-view. So I set out to discredit him – a relatively easy thing to do, given his shaky historicity.

Even now, I take the gospel accounts of his life, death and resurrection with a grain of salt. I'm quite aware that they were all written decades after the fact, giving that fact more than enough time to be born again as fiction. I fully acknowledge that Jesus, if he once existed, may have been a deluded fool who gambled and lost. I can also live with the possibility that he never existed at all in the usual sense, but represents a compilation of human hopes and yearnings and dreams.

I well remember the moment that last possibility occurred to me. Much as I congratulated myself on my cleverness, I felt afraid. At first I told myself this was most likely the kind of fear a child feels on discovering Santa Claus isn't 'real'. But later I realized it was a very adult fear. An ancient fear.

I am speaking of the awe we feel in the presence of a mythical figure. One who has stepped out of history into story. Out of time into eternity.

I had killed Jesus with my intellect, only to have him rise again in my imagination. And that's the one place this fiction writer will never be able to turf him out of.

* * *

Meanwhile, back in the tomb ...

I got here by pushing my own envelope of assumptions about how much I could do and how far I could go. I'm pretty sure God approves of envelope-pushing (though sometimes has funny ways of showing it).

When I emerge from this 'tomb', it will be as something else. Even if I go on writing short fiction, I will write differently. A step has been taken, and must not be taken back. Even to try to do so would be sinful – a word I very seldom use.

For now, all I can do is wait in the dark and try to remember that with the grace of God even a stone can move. Try to believe that the moment will come when a sliver of light will start to show along its edge.

---

1. *The Book of Common Prayer,* Anglican Church of Canada (1962), 71.

2. Luke 9:51.

3. Letter from John Metcalf to K.D. Miller, September 25, 1995.

The Most Wonderful Game in the World

JOHN METCALF

My father was a Methodist minister, my mother a rigid and pietistic elementary school teacher. I grew up in the north of England in a society both narrow and grim. I went to church morning and evening on Sundays and also went to church functions during the week. This kind of growing up was not as cut off as, say, a Mennonite or Amish upbringing but there were analogies. I suggest something of this upbringing in a novella called *Private Parts: A Memoir*.

My brother and I were fortunate to go to superb academic grammar schools where we were worked like slaves. These schools offered us a vision of a possible future far removed from the thin gruel of Methodism with its repressive attitudes towards sex, its anti-intellectualism, its comfy ignorance.

During my later childhood and adolescence I came to see my father's religion – and its social application – as the enemy to be fought. I came to see that I would only survive intact emotionally and sexually if I escaped from everything my parents held most dear. During this period I was reading endlessly in literature, history, theology and art. My deepest emotional experiences were in music – mainly traditional jazz – and in painting and literature. Painters, it seemed to me, had the right ideas about life's possibilities, spendthrift when possible, firm-fleshed women, absinthe in the afternoon.

At this time, too, language began to haunt me. I understood certain words as magical, as incantation. I've written about this in an essay called 'Lieutenant Lúkaš's Cat'. I was ravished by the literature I was studying in school. I was enraptured by the literature I was reading on

---

Ottawa author and editor John Metcalf is one of sixteen writers who responded to my questionnaire concerning the spiritual aspects of the writing life. His was one of four responses I chose to reproduce in full.

my own – poetry mainly – a hodgepodge of the Imagists, H.D., Pound, Eliot, D.H. Lawrence, Flecker, Dylan Thomas, Auden, Gerard Manley Hopkins.

This joy in art and literature has intensified over the years. I live now a secular version of my father's life. I've often thought about whether or not I could be considered 'religious'. At one time I might have passed muster as a pantheist but that seems to have ebbed. I've been known to make arguments claiming that history itself is sacred. In a circle of standing stones or in the shadow of a menhir I've been known to speak of numina, and to advance the possibility of immanence. But this is, I'm afraid, simply me being pompous and emotionally sloppy, wistful for a belief I lack. I do have strong feelings both for the natural world and for the past but I suspect that everything is, at base, not a belief in immanence at all but simply a feeling, a purely aesthetic response.

Some have argued that an aesthetic response *is* a spiritual response but I think that's an argument advanced by people without religious belief who want some kind of solace, something larger than themselves to cling to. I think the aesthetic as divine is delusional.

It is also an abstraction. The aesthetic always drives us back to things made, to words crafted. It connects us to the real world, to the makers of things in the real world. It connects us more firmly with the human.

When I was younger, I used to argue that art had a moral function. Now, I'm far less sure of that. I think I still believe that art has a moral *effect* simply by making people more complicated, more refined emotionally. But my thinking about art in the last few years has narrowed. Or possibly deepened. I'm slowly coming to see – at least, I think I am – that great art is essentially a game. The most wonderful game in the world. The rules of the game are not written out anywhere; they are dimly apprehended by the players and spectators. When a player wins in the game, however, the victory is obvious to all and is shared by all.

We know – or we can come to know through years of looking and touching – that we are seeing a victory in the game in that white Sung bowl, in a print by Hokusai, in a Bambara *chi-wara* mask, in a bust by Bernini, in a Eudora Welty story.

These victories in the game are not, I think, manifestations of the divine. Rather, they are *human* triumphs. Our players have created something which did not exist in the world before. In very complex ways, which we'll probably never be able to explain fully, some artists make things which fill us with joy. And it is a very special kind of joy. It is unlike anything else we feel. And each victory becomes part of us and helps to define who we are. Each victory in the game adds to us and changes the possibility of what we might become. And what others who come after us can become. And this has been going on since before the wonderful animals painted in the Lascaux caves and the red and ochre animals and palm prints painted on the rocks in the Sahara by people of whom we have no record.

If I believe anything which nudges towards the idea of God, I believe we're held in a great net of history and that we are a part of a continuity which shapes us and which artists help to shape.

Evensong

The other night a woman I once worked with on a church committee phoned to ask if I would help with something having to do with the parish. As usual, I felt both flattered and dismayed. And I heard myself say, as a reason for refusing, that I'm rethinking my relationship with my church.

Sometimes my mouth knows what's going on before the rest of me does. I was reminded of a similar moment, over a decade ago, long before it had occurred to me to darken the door of a church, when I heard myself tell a colleague that writing is the way I pray.

Well, I guess I *am* rethinking my relationship with my church. Not quitting – not yet, anyway, and maybe never. I'm fairly sure I will always believe in God. I know I will always be imaginatively nourished by the Jesus story. But when it comes to my parish church, my denomination, maybe the very act of churchgoing, it's time to step back and take a critical (and equally self-critical) look.

At one time, I did volunteer work, dropped in regularly to Coffee Hour and couldn't get in or out the doors of the place without making half a dozen brief connections. But I discovered that involving myself in church activities, however commendable those activities might be, distracted me from the very thing I was hoping to do by attending a worship service, namely worship.

This is all very personal, of course. Other people manage to balance faith and works; indeed, for many parishioners, faith *is* works. But again, I'm a writer, and we tend to be essentially solitary souls. Also, mine is a large enough and busy enough congregation that if one person chooses to step back, another will always choose to step forward. Some might find this alienating, in much the way they find big, busy cities alienating. But I like the big city. I like the option it gives me of seeking out company or losing myself in the crowd. I would be as uncomfortable in a touchy-feely congregation where I was prayed for aloud by name as I would be in a small town where everybody knew my business.

So why do I join with a faith community in worshipping God week after week? This is a question I've asked myself elsewhere in this book. I'll probably continue to ask it as long as I continue to go to church. In fact, the question has become more urgent as a result of writing these essays, and the answer more elusive. What I actually believe, of course, does come into it. And that's another question I've been asking myself, one way and another.

In the following attempt to articulate that belief, my purpose is neither to proselytize nor to convert my reader. It's more like a personal inventory-taking. Except there seems to be a discrepancy between what I have in stock and what I'm supposed to have, according to the Creed in the *Book of Common Prayer:*

I believe in one God the Father Almighty, Maker of heaven and earth, And of all things visible and invisible.[1]

Paternalistic viewpoint, quaint capitalization and seventeenth-century cosmology aside, yes, I can go along with that much.

And in one Lord Jesus Christ, the only-begotten Son of God, Begotten of the Father before all worlds; God, of God; Light, of Light; Very God, of very God; Begotten, not made; Being of one substance with the Father; Through whom all things were made.

Though the purpose here is to elucidate, in fact things are starting to get murky. I am not unaware of the social and historical impact of the writing of both the Creed and the *Book of Common Prayer.* Both were acts of faith and courage on the part of the church fathers. The Creed was an attempt to give people words with which to express their beliefs, and the BCP to put their religion literally into their hands. But there is a point where articulation hardens into rote. The above citation reminds me of a theological check list being ticked off item by item. The social and political issues that at one time rendered each word a manifesto have been largely forgotten. Now, the list is dreary and wearying. So much easier just to mumble through and try not to think.

Who for us men and for our salvation came down from heaven, And was incarnate by the Holy Ghost of the Virgin Mary, And was made man.

As a matter of fact, I do believe in the incarnation. I do believe God was, is and evermore shall be, made human. With all due respect to my parents, I believe that *I* was incarnate by the Holy Ghost of the Virgin Mary. I believe everyone reading this book was too, be they Christian, Jewish, Muslim, Hindu, Wiccan or atheist. This is not Christian imperialism on my part. I'm simply trying to say that I believe God enters into every part of God's creation. And in my attempt to do so, I'm using the 'language' that is my spiritual mother tongue – metaphors drawn from a story that I learned by heart before I could read or write. Were I a non-Christian, I would speak a different spiritual language and tell a different story. But I would, on some level at least, be saying essentially the same thing.

And was crucified also for us under Pontius Pilate.

Pontius Pilate is complacency. Convenience. The status quo. The boat that must not be rocked. We can *all* be crucified under Pontius Pilate. At any moment of any day, we can choose whether or not to crucify ourselves and each other as Pontius Pilate. As a writer, I can sit back the way Pilate does and airily ask 'What is truth?' or I can take up that truth and carry it to Calvary.

He suffered and was buried, And the third day he rose again according to the Scriptures, And ascended into heaven, And sitteth on the right hand of the Father.

As I have stated elsewhere in this book, I do not believe in a literal, physical Resurrection. This does not mean that I refuse to sing 'Jesus Christ is risen today' on Easter Sunday morning. Quite the contrary. It's one of my favourite hymns, and one of my favourite moments of the year. Because I do believe in rebirth – in a continuous cycle of birth, death and rebirth in fact, throughout one's lifetime. As a writer, I must experience these little Bethlehems and Calvaries over and over in order to grow. And everything I have ever written reaches a point in its development that I can only describe as Gethsemane, where it must choose either the safe road or the one that leads to the court of Pontius Pilate.

And he shall come again with glory to judge both the quick and the dead: Whose kingdom shall have no end.

Eschatological statements of any kind tend to remind me of *Star Wars* movies. As a child, I used to study with morbid fascination Michelangelo's painting of the Last Judgement. I remember the expression on the face of one poor chap being pulled by the legs down into hell. He is clutching handfuls of his own hair in what looks like grief for his lost chances and regret for his sins. (Though a wicked part of my imagination gives him the caption: 'Shoot! I could have had a V-8!') But

I don't think I've ever quite believed in hell. An after-the-fact hell, that is. I think we manufacture our own, right here and now, by making temples of our malls, gods of our celebrities and a soul-destroying liturgy of our perpetual distraction.

And I believe in the Holy Ghost, the Lord, the Giver of Life, Who proceedeth from the Father and the Son, Who with the Father and the Son together is worshipped and glorified, Who spake by the Prophets.

If anything is going to convert me to Unitarianism, it will be that statement. I've never been able to take the Holy Ghost seriously. For one thing, his timing is lousy. He shows up at Pentecost, which is weeks after Easter. This links him in my mind with that hapless juggler who had to follow the Beatles on the Ed Sullivan Show back in 1963. But there's something else, too. If I've got it right, the Holy Ghost is the *memory* or *lasting influence* of Jesus' sojourn on earth. The spirit of Christianity, in other words, which is supposed to live on in individual Christians and in the Christian church. Well, okay. But again, I would like to see the whole concept opened up. I'm even beginning to question the necessity of a person's being baptized before they can receive Communion. (To its credit, my church is also starting to raise this question.) It all depends, I guess, on how exclusive and conditional we want things to be. And once more, my mouth knew what was going on in my head before the rest of me did. A year or so ago, during the passing of the Peace, when we turn and shake hands with our pew mates, I heard myself saying not 'The Peace of Christ', but simply, 'Peace be with you'.

And I believe One, Holy, Catholic and Apostolic Church. I acknowledge one Baptism for the remission of sins. And I look for the Resurrection of the dead, And the Life of the world to come. Amen.

I neither know nor care what is going to happen when the sun finally burns out. Meanwhile, whenever my religion starts getting imperialistic and exclusionary, it loses me. I live in Toronto in the year 2001. I can no more believe that my Jewish friend or my Muslim colleague or my atheist relative is damned for not accepting Jesus as their personal saviour than I can seriously clap for Tinkerbell.

So why do I keep on going to church? Because *I believe in one God.* There. That's my Creed. Because through accidents of birth and upbringing I am bent into a vaguely Judaeo-Christian shape. Because the cycle of the Christian year – Advent, Christmas, Lent, Easter,

Pentecost – appeal to me as an artist by reminding me of the cycle of birth, death and rebirth. Because the music and liturgy of the service give me something that is increasingly hard to find in a society that is casual to the point of being brutal, namely ritual.

Ritual is a prime ingredient of my writing life. I have a room for writing set aside in my apartment, and a time of day when, almost without fail, I can be found there. On one wall there is a Celtic cross. Tacked to the bulletin board there is a dried and curling palm leaf. I get a fresh leaf every Palm Sunday, let it crisp all year in my study, then take it back to church the Sunday before Ash Wednesday, where it is burned. Three days later, ash from the burning of my leaf and hundreds of others is dabbed in the shape of a cross onto my forehead by a priest who reminds me, 'From dust you came and to dust you will return.' There is a sense of completion in that moment that I find strangely comforting.

In the corner above my desk there is a small wooden bracket supporting a tiny plastic Saint Jude. Though I'm not really into saints, Jude appeals to me as the patron of things lost, things despaired of, and hopeless causes in general. I get a kick out of writing beneath his watchful eye. I like to imagine him catching and keeping safe for me all those wonderful ideas, phrases and words that flit in and out of my mind too swiftly for me to get them down on paper.

It is no accident that the only physical manifestations of my faith (besides the small gold cross I wear around my neck) are clustered in this particular room where I write. It makes me wonder if, in time, this room will become my only 'church' and this act of writing my only 'worship'.

If so, I really don't think God will suffer for it. But I can't help wondering if I will.

---

1. All citations are from the *Book of Common Prayer* of the Anglican Church of Canada (1962), pages 71–72.

Acknowledgements

Some of the essays in *Holy Writ* were previously published. 'Morning Prayer' first appeared in the Summer 1999 issue of *The Lazy Writer*. 'Easter Egg' and a portion of 'Whit's End' were published in *The New Quarterly*, Summer 2000. 'Travels with Harold' appeared in *Canadian Notes & Queries*, Fall & Winter 2000.

K.D. Miller was born in Hamilton, Ontario, and graduated from the University of British Columbia with a Master of Fine Arts in theatre. Her stories and essays have appeared in numerous magazines and have been nominated for the Journey Prize and the National Magazine Award for fiction (1997). In 1999 she was a runner-up in the PRISM *international* short fiction contest. Two collections of her stories have been published – *A Litany in Time of Plague* (PQL 1994), and *Give Me Your Answer* (PQL 1999) – with the latter being short-listed for the Upper Canada Brewing Company's inaugural Writers' Craft Award and the sixteenth annual TORGI Talking Book of the Year Award.